LOVE
GROAN

School of Love
Trilogy

School of Love

&

University of Love
parts 1 & 2

Tom Fry

Love Groan
School of Love Trilogy

This edition 2021

ISBN 978-0-9545512-8-5

Published by
Pi Brand Books
London, UK

Amazon Books
© 2021

School of Love
First published Kindle & paperback 2018
Pi Brand Books/Amazon Books
This edition 2021
Copyright © Tom Fry, 2018

University of Love, pt.1
First published Kindle & paperback 2018
Pi Brand Books/Amazon Books
This edition 2021
Copyright © Tom Fry, 2018

University of Love, pt.2
First published Kindle & paperback 2019
Pi Brand Books/Amazon Books
This edition 2021
Copyright © Tom Fry, 2019

© 2018 © 2019 © 2021 Tom Fry

for Diana Keane
with heartfelt thanks
decades late

Contents vii

Introduction xi

School of Love

Groan From Seed

University of Love, part 1

University of Love, part 2

Dear reader,

This is my freely given testimony.

All the characters are real and perhaps still walking around in the world at this time.

No names are named, litigation has never appealed.

You are forewarned that this is not a light piece of prose, nay, this is the heaviest burden of a long-troubled soul, penned with the cathartic release of public declaration in mind.

A series of chastening experiences; gory personal details of loves and heartaches, an exploration of root causes and flowing effects, that which is real within a mind and without one, stark realisations and good old plain ignorance.

These memories are my truth, the very fabric of my reality, a one-size-fits-all autobiographical therapy to quell recent indelicate stirrings of previously deeply-buried emotion, nought more than an attempt to recapture the flush of youthful moods before circumstance prevents the freedom to do so, or age should take them from me.

By writing this, I don't want to embarrass anyone very much, charge anyone with indecent behaviour, nor admit to improper behaviour. I've no desire to create waves, undermine anyone, refute any movement, deny anyone their reality, kick up a stink, rub noses in it, knock heads, or head up a manhunt with peasants, pikes and pitchforks. None of that, I don't have the energy. I figure that stuff happens anyway, so, go with it.

History is stored in stories. We each have our story. This story is my history. Maybe history will be kind. Maybe not. I'm not going to further waste your time by attempting to justify it. I stand by it all, the whole shebang.

As a monkey throwing poo at a piano, hopefully some of it will strike a chord.

Tom Fry

School of Love

—

Groan From Seed

SCHOOL OF LOVE

1: In the Beginning

She was my childhood sweetheart; she liked me, I liked her, everyone knew it. Every day I longed to see her. Our houses were nearby, so, after school and at weekends, we would hang out in the street, flirting endlessly without boredom.

She was faultless; playful, pretty, kind, smiley and happy, with a dirty chuckle that made me laugh. At junior school she'd be the only one to ever hunt me down in kiss chase. She bought me enormous Easter eggs. We'd share straws. Once, on a sports day, she grabbed my goolies.

If ever there was the one, she was the one. All of my first sexual thoughts and damp dreams were dreamed of her. None before her had been so fondly contemplated with such a flood of chemicals in the blood to play with. In my young uncluttered mind, body and soul, I liked, loved and lusted her more than anyone could have liked, loved and lusted anything. She was my goddess. We were destined.

Senior school was upon us, we weren't just kids any more. They split us into different classes, in their wisdom, but we found each other in every break-time at our special meeting spot.

There was no need to 'ask her out' because it was known, it just *was*, we only had to agree to a day and an activity, however, we weren't yet allowed out into town on our own. We asked permission from our parents to go to the cinema, they agreed, but only if we went with friends. I argued that she and I *were* friends, but, despite all protests, my first ever date was, at the whim of my loving parents, unfortunately, a double date, two boys and two girls.

We went on a Saturday for the early showing of a romantic film about death and pottery. Certificate twelve.

My friend turned up, late, and we walked into town both anxious of interactions soon to happen. The girls were also arriving together; we were going to meet them outside, but once we'd arrived, they were already inside watching the adverts.

I nervously approached the desk and asked for my ticket. How old are you? *Um, twelve.* And your friend. I'm eleven. *No, you just turned twelve.* No, I'm eleven. *No,* he's twelve. No, he's not. Yes, he is. No, he's not, he just said he's eleven. Yes, well, he only just turned twelve. No, really, I'm not twelve, I'm definitely eleven. Nnnnnngh, okay, so, um, what else is on?

We bought two tickets and went in to see a cartoon musical about a mermaid finding her legs. The craggy usher made sure that we found our screen when it looked like we were going to make a sneaky dash for it.

My friend was a very best friend, but he was a prized pillock. That day, we didn't meet the girls at all. I felt sorely resentful that external factors had got in the way of *my* happiness; parents, friend, and film-classification-board, so made myself deeply miserable about it, determinedly, in the classic pre-teenage kind of a way. Annoyed with him, we fell out for weeks as I stropped and sulked, but mates are mates, so after a while it became funny, though more to him than me.

She was not happy with me for the first time, and the root-cause not mine to control. Injustice and embarrassment burned as fiercely as any soul set on fire for the first time will blaze.

We tried again a month later, disappointingly, another double date, this time we were definitely going to meet outside. Definitely definitely. I took a different friend. *He* insisted that we all see a horror movie about a fear of spiders, and then refused to sit next to the girls, but at least we all got in together.

We boys sat side by side in the row directly behind the girls and threw popcorn at them in the tense bits.

At this point, I'd run out of likely friends. As had she.

2: God Created the Heaven

My childhood goddess and I were ready to take the next step. Our first kiss had been four or five exciting years in the making. Peer pressures had finally forced the issue, a time was set, word got out, everyone gathered in the usual crush, as they do when such an event happens in an upstairs school corridor.

There she was, fidgeting nervously, the diamond in a ring of her very best friends; gorgeous to behold in her senior school uniform, short skirt, short tie, warm sunlight twinkling upon her perfect auburn hair. Here I was too, shining brightly from the inside, kipper tie straightened and hair all messy.

I took it all in, absorbing the entire surroundings. Every shout of encouragement, each friendly taunt. The air trembled, a hush descended. I focused in on her, every micro-emotion and empathic look, each tiny dimple-twitch captured forever on my retinas in super-slow-motion. We looked at each other. We smiled at each other. We each took a tentative step towards each other. We took another tentative step. Cheers went up, a chant started. Kiss her kiss her, from the boys, kiss him kiss him, from the girls. Blood pumping, my vibe would've felled giants. Indestructible, and sick as a dog. I breathed deeply to calm the trembling, once more taking in the enormity of the moment for what it was. Another tentative step and smile. Another. She held out her hand to take mine, I reached out, took a push in the back, forgot where my feet were, stumbled forward and head-butted her in the chin with a loud crack.

She ran off, as one would. Her friends helped me up from the floor, and then knocked me to the floor for ruining her perfect moment. Through their skirted legs, obscured, corridor double doors swung glumly shut on a last glimpse of her buckled shoes.

And that was pretty much the last time I ever saw her. There were other reasons. One such reason being the school goalkeeper, who'd managed to get his life together enough to leave the street where he lived without a chaperone, and could kiss girls without hospitalising them.

I was told, unhelpfully, that, by God's grace, out there, *some*where, out *there* in the big wide world, there would be a life-partner for everyone. One partner each. Hooray. But, that didn't help at all. If anything, it meant that it was doubly hard to contemplate letting her go. If we were only allowed one, then I'd already used up my quotient. It didn't seem very fair. It seemed as if God hadn't really thought this through very well.

She remained haunting my dreams as the golden goddess I'd always imagined her as, yet, physically, in the real world, so it transpired, she was not mine to behold. She had moved on.

Dreamscape allowed me to continue my childhood fantasy of an uncorrupted world, as I saw it, reality only half as real. Waking up was as being sucked through an infinitely tiny hole into an eerie alternative place where everything was identical, except for her eternal betrothal to the school goalie.

Silently, impotently, yielding to fate, I fumed jealously over a woman for the very first time, found a shell, retreated into it, and that, as they say, was that.

3: And the Earth

Rude alarm clocks halted the nightly horrors that chased me through exhausting dreams. Consciousness beat back the Demons with all the gritty fortitude of a child. Daily morning newspaper delivery meant a much-needed hour alone with thoughts and freedom of the deserted local streets. My bike and I were one, wobbling up the lamp-lit roads fully-laden in all weathers.

At home, my parents made time for me every day. My mother nurtured, fed and counselled, my father guided homework and musical practice. My sister did her thing. A happy home habitat.

School continued apace. I picked up the nickname Baldy, achieved academic successes, nearly joined a clever club but didn't, boarding school was proposed and half-heartedly declined because I didn't want to break up God's perfect family unit. I got 'good' at ping-pong, switched up from 'cello to the double-bass and joined a youth orchestra. I felt lucky, and, truly, I was.

A local opera house needed pre-pubescent kids for Puccini. It happens. They'd picked our school because the school choir had won awards. Luckily for me, all of the choir had already been nabbed for a London show which they went up to do most evenings. We were the artsy leftovers, the musical scraps.

Two schools were doing it, in case of serious illness. Eight kids from each. Four boys and four girls. The show used only six. We competed for places and tour dates between us. As understudy to our soloist, my main stage duty was to bring in a box, brightly, for an adult to jump onto and warble upon. Vital.

Socially, the girls from my school knew about and teased me for my past kissing efforts, just the once, which is plenty enough indignity, thanks. Blushing and ashamed in their presence, they were off my radar.

From the other school, there were new girls who brought me out of my shell, girls I wasn't humiliated in front of, beautiful talented dynamic girls that didn't squint and smirk at internal memory when they saw me. I noticed those girls and knew they were very special. One particularly caught my eye, she reminded me of me; religious, caught in the headlights of a world which she couldn't compute. Through rehearsals I'd vie for her attentions, as a chimp might. When rehearsals were finished with, it looked like we would never meet again.

I was delighted that I'd started to find other girls attractive, even if we weren't predestined. Distracted with the possibility of there being only the one partner each in the world, split attentions and affections created ethical problems to tackle and grapple with. Although pleased and blessed to be living through the difficult process of understanding human nature, muddled concepts of; destiny, fate, free will, free love, marriage, divorce and bigamy, confused my tiny-weeny mind.

Our school group assembled at the train station to leave for the last weekend away. I was the first one to arrive, dropped early with a heavy suitcase by a working parent. Hours passed slowly as the usuals turned up in dribs and drabs, when shock, there *she* was, a replacement for the tour, my heart fluttered and I lost all voice and breathing for several minutes. She was coming with us. The best of possibilities had transpired. I'd been given another chance to make meaningful connection. God had blessed me personally with this gift of opportunity.

Suddenly, just as it was time to leave, the chaperone noticed that too many boys had turned up, and, though it could be proved that we all had it scheduled on our rotas, they hadn't planned for tickets or hotel rooms. The substitute argued that he hadn't had a decent run at it, which he had, the soloist claimed that he was the soloist, which he was, the other quiet boy stayed quiet and it was put onto me to give up my place for the substitute.

I couldn't rightfully announce that God had chosen this weekend for me to spend time with my future wife. The choice was: to be selfish and seize the day, or to be kind and miss life's actual opportunity. The trousers of time split wide open at the crutch.

Two minutes later, the train departed.

Ten minutes later, I stopped staring at the bend in the track where the train had been.

Half an hour later, I'd spent most of my money on fast food.

Over an hour later, at home with my suitcase, lamentations came in a splenetic spate of pissy prayers, appeals and pleas.

I went to bed early and upset, cursing all impure decisions I'd ever made, pleading with my God to forgive me for masturbating, or whatever it was that I'd done to deserve such divine torment.

She appeared in my dreams that night, briefly, quietly, before leaving the glow of my campfire and wandering off out of sight into the darkness. I chased her trail vainly through the pulsating Esher dimensions, but she was gone, vanished, near but nowhere, hopelessly absent or hidden behind an unthinkable thought. Hollow solitude drowned me in my skin. Little boy lost in an infinite infinity of infinities.

The following school day, my form tutor sent me to the headmaster's office for skiving. I wasn't having that, so I gave both emotional barrels and left the office feeling much better.

Upon the singers' return from their operatic weekend away, the soloist said that he'd kissed the girl from the other school when they'd played spin the bottle. I refused to believe him because the very contemplation of the thought hurt deeply.

I invited my golden goddess back into a lonely dreamscape. It seemed all too clear that I'd received God's direct instruction to lead me back to my one truly true preordained path.

If only my one truly truest love wasn't currently occupied snogging the school goalkeeper.

SCHOOL OF LOVE

4: And the Earth Was Without Form

On tour with the county youth orchestra, I was a burbling mess, rarely did they take such juveniles, and for good reason. We were abroad in Europe. Being socially thick and unaware, I got into trouble for heading out with the older kids without telling anyone where I'd gone. I took my dressing-down stood in front of the full-orchestra, whilst staring forlornly at my feet.

That evening one of the older girls, pouty lipped, voluptuous and stunning, pushed me into one of the bedrooms and closed the door on the noisy party behind us. Obviously a little sorry for me, and a little drunk, after a little chat, she asked me if I wanted to kiss. And yes, I did. She was out of my league, exceedingly pretty, almost a woman, of course I wanted to kiss.

I'd only recently promised my mum that I'd never grow up; suddenly here I was in a bedroom in a foreign country with a fully developed lady staring me deeply in the eyes. Ooooo.

While she relaxed onto the bed teasing me tenderly, I sat on the edge and twiddled tensely, giggling with excruciating happinesses. For five glorious minutes bliss knew no bounds as we positioned ourselves, gave up, laughed, repositioned, smiled, giggled, observed, laughed, gave up and tried again.

Okay, stop, I want to kiss, seriously now, this is my first kiss, I want to get this right. Come here then. Okay, what do I do? Just hold me here. Okay. And here. Okay. Now, just kiss me.

Pausing, I hesitated with heart aflutter, then slowly, very *very* slowly leaned my gawky neck in with lustful intent when my sister barged into the room brashly and broke the spell, sat down heavily on the bed between us and demanded that we returned to the party, which we did.

Dreams were stressful, and that was that.

5: And Void

In the final years of school, the girl from the opera, who'd previously left my dreams so sadly and hopelessly, had moved locally and joined our school. At first, having barely glimpsed her in busy corridors, I was sure that she was just a trick of the mind, wishful thinking made flesh. But, no, it turned out, she *was* real, *there* she was. Uuuurgh nana nernyer. Every time I saw her, rushing this way and that, I'd feel nauseous and have trouble breathing. I spoke barely three garbled words to her in weeks, which, in itself, was an extreme effort of courage and will.

She entered my dreams once more, only to remain lost, silent and unobtainable, hiding between the nether dimensions. There was a universe calling to me, now here and yet nowhere, at once everywhere and all things, but nowhere and nothing. Chaos, causality and casual accident, snarling at each other.

A hook, trailing in unseen gases far out beyond my ken, couldn't bring worlds close enough to connect or get purchase. Frustration rose. The Mr Tickle conundrum, which turns children inside out while adapting to a lack of magical powers, became a multi-dimensional knot of infinite arms tying the body into this reality by its tangled mass of overlapped densely-packed otherworldly hyper-flesh. Heavy was my achey-breaky heart.

Curious, I thought, if this *was* an angel made flesh she'd know my intention. I stopped masturbating as a sign of respect to her, in hope it would improve the spiritual imbalance between us. I slacked a little after a while but it was my offering to God most of the time. From what I saw, it didn't seem likely that she'd noticed me, but that's exactly the way an angel would behave, demure, then, out of the blue, they save your goddamn soul. That's how it worked with angels. I was very certain of unreality.

After more weeks and months, I still couldn't get her out of my head, or, indeed, into my dreams. Trapped in indecision, I couldn't work out whether this was God taunting me again, or if this was finally an offering of peace and goodwill to all men, after so many despairingly desperate calls for it.

At a multi-school event in a high-vaulted theatre foyer, students started mixing in a break. I'd been playing the double-bass in the combined orchestra and was just putting it down and slackening off the bow when she came over to speak to me. So super-excited I didn't know what to say, I garbled something, she didn't seem to mind too much, I swung my leg over the double-bass and pretended to ride it like a horse, she seemed to laugh, this was going well, I asked her if she was singing in the choir and she opened her mouth to speak.

Of all people, my father was in the room and he loomed up from directly behind her as only fathers can. He interrupted her thoughts to give me a stern warning about mucking about and treating my instrument with respect. By the time I looked up from my feet, she had gone.

I saw her again in corridors, ever hopeful of her approach and sicker than a puking pig, but we'd returned to the swiftly moving cliques that kept us dashing past each other so hastily.

I didn't make any grandiose displays of romantic affection, assuming this would only upset the natural order of things. If it were the *will* of God, then she *will* come to me, I thought. She entered dreamscape as reachable, permitted into my campfire when I called. Some subtle change had nudged her half rotation back into view, I could witness her energy. Images of her face stored as rare snippets to rewind, play over, and interact with, we'd have a too short a moment of bliss, if we were quick, before my dad's shadow energy would show up and lurk menacingly. There were dark, terrifying, anxious, stressful nightmares, but they were dealt with, eventually, with a little prayer and fortitude.

.

I started wanking again and dismissed ideas of the psychophysical unity of our two beings in the world. I liked wanking, very much. Guilt and shame concerning visualisations of her body were bearable, only if our souls weren't to be tied together for eternity. As dry weeks passed without new footage available, her fading image a priceless memory stretched thin through overuse, it became apparent that all the moments spent bobbing about waving at her in corridors combined, weren't half as satisfying as two minutes with some privacy and a dirty thought. One minute would do. Or less.

There was one more surprise meeting, years later. She was alone at the same station platform where a train had taken her away the first time. I waited on the concourse, watching to see if she would get on, or if, once again, the malevolent fates would be clacking our playing pieces together with evil glee only to throw them back across the board, trapping my piece uselessly under an iron brick of shyness. She climbed aboard, now was my chance. After a bit of dithering about whether I should be perving over her, I plucked up the courage and entered through the same door, she sat in the compartment at the end. I pulled the door, entered the carriage and sat on the edge of the opposite seat breathing lightly. After a short hello, hello, howdy, howdy, that was it, no more breath. As the oxygen ran out, so did I, grabbing at the handle and scuttling off down the corridor shaking. I didn't go back and left her alone.

The provenance of the situation had flattened all sensible rationale and inflated panic until the brain burst. I didn't have the courage to face my angel after what I'd done to her in my mind. Her soul would never forgive me when we got to heaven if I made a pass at her in this life. Maybe no more angels will come into my existence, maybe this really was going to be it now, but I'd made my bed, and I'd be lying if I said the sheets weren't crispy.

SCHOOL OF LOVE

6: And Darkness *Was* Upon the Face of the Deep

Senior school rolled on. In the fifth and final year, I received an expensive Valentine's card, with no idea who it was from. A capital letter and partial second letter had been crossed out as a clue to a name. I suspected a wind-up, but none of my friends had enough money or malice to buy a thing like that as a prank.

I sat with it for a few days before following the clue to several girls, no, no, no way, *maybe*. It seemed likely that a girl I'd met a few times through town church meet-ups had sent it. Of all walks of life available to have chosen, it was important to her to find someone within: The Christian Flock, at least, that's what I gleaned from her mum when she caught me coming out of school that week, giving me reason to believe that the whole thing might well have been her mum's idea from the off.

Twas all a bit sudden, taking on this squirmy information, I barely knew her. I felt I'd been unfairly shortlisted on a list that I really didn't want to be on. Love should be a two-way street or the street should be closed, that's what *my* jealous broodings had summarised. Of course, this is not to deny daydreams contemplating what life would be like with all girls encountered; in church, in school, in orchestras, in all life, my equally viable shortlist of potential partners, imagining what our kids would look like, how they'd turn out, all of it. I could only presume that these rolling thoughts were how other people dealt with their isolated brooding realities too, it was just somewhat overwhelming to realise that I myself could be that imagined future for someone else. My mini-mind wasn't quite capable of taking that in from any but my own heart's chosen desire. Fussily, I didn't want her to be my first kiss, and when it all came to a head, in one form or another, I told her as much.

It wasn't quite that easy though, firstly she refused to confirm that the card was from her, then she tried to get me to admit, by the by, if I'd want to kiss her exceedingly attractive friend, which I did, obviously, then she asked if I wanted to kiss her. You can see the problem. She stormed off crying while still not having confirmed that the card was from her. The truth was that I didn't fancy her as much as her friend but had still thought her pleasant and quite pretty enough, there might have been some mileage in it if we'd've hung out and become friends, but, crucially, it was her herself who made comparison between her and her very attractive friend, not me, she did it to herself.

I suspected that she had her community's vision of perfect personal purity hounding her dreams. I felt awful for her, but it wasn't my duty to kiss her. If she'd been direct, I'd've weighed it up and maybe after a week or two thought yes, maybe, but she'd put pay to that by cloak and dagger situational control and emotional nonsense. She'd needed me to deny her friend's beauty and declare undying love from the start as a sign of God's will, I knew that one, I'd made that bargain a few times myself, but I'm no angel, I knew *that* much. Angel's don't masturbate.

I felt very strongly that I should be allowed the same basic freedom to choose my destiny as anyone else. When alone, drunk on the heady whine of self-righteousness, I wielded my first rejection as a mighty conceptual battle-axe, learning a lot about openness, directness, truth, lies, and the value of speaking one's mind. A stopper had been pulled at the base of my neck and brain-liquid sloshed over my organs. It felt good being master of my own destiny in *any* capacity. The power of 'no'.

A few years later, via the mother network, I heard that she'd been badly affected by an eating disorder. There is no doubting my part to blame for this, even though unaware of her feelings until one week before she decided to never speak to me again. Guilt exists within when looking for it, but it's not too strong.

7: And the Spirit of God Moved Upon the Face of the Waters

Before exams had started, a tall, very pretty girl showed some shy romantic interest. She had train-track braces, and so wasn't overly fussed about kissing. She didn't make me sick with nerves, and she wanted someone to make her feel special.

After months of gentle flirting in corridors, I fell for her, but, I didn't love her, for, despite constant welcome distractions, my heart pondered wistfully the purest of passions still borne for others, there couldn't have been enough love in the galaxy leftover to share with anyone else. Yet, much to my surprise, this new girl thrust herself into a dream wearing suggestive burnished Valkyrie garb, fought with my golden goddess and won the battle of mind's affection. She then kindly approached for fantasy bio-mechanicals, exploding my defensive bulwark.

It seemed that bio-chemically I had been given the grace to move on. I looked within and found that there was, perhaps, just enough space in this raggedy heart to love again. Perhaps.

School swimming gala rolled by, we spent all day hanging out pretty much naked. Her race came up, so she disappeared for a bit, when she reappeared she no longer had the towel hiding her form, slinking along the side of the pool in a one-piece. My jaw hit the floor as I got that tingle of lust that had so far been the unique privilege of dreamscape. She swam her race and promptly returned to the stand where I sat crippled with a stiffy, the likes of which bend whole universes around them.

I was now, officially, in love. Certainly in lust.

My race prep-time was called, so I hobbled off, pretending I'd hurt my back. I got to the changing rooms. Minutes passed. It wouldn't go away. I tried hitting it. Nothing. I tried bashing it against things. Nothing. Nature was speaking and I had to listen.

With my towel carefully positioned, I shuffled poolside, told the teacher I'd injured myself and returned to the stands still bent over. When she quizzed me, I told her exactly why. She laughed and laughed and I wasn't embarrassed. Telling the truth with humour seemed to be a fine way of making connection.

It all seemed right, I'd set my mind straight, I'd told her I fancied her, knew she liked me, but I had no bottle to 'ask her out'. Flustered and fearful in front of her feminine friends, a few faltering efforts failed fruitlessly. Things dragged on falteringly.

It appeared that I would miss my window of opportunity, when a faint rumour on the rumour wheel reignited the action. It was said that a friend of mine, the soloist in the opera, no less, was planning to beat me to it. I wasn't having that, so I ran to find her as fast as my accursed sprouting legs would carry me.

Winded, managing acute stitch and thudding growing pains, physically falling down in front of her, I 'asked her out' grimacing breathlessly, as if styling out the end of a cheesy rom-com. I felt that I'd made a good choice in overcoming fear with physical comedy. She said yes. We hugged shyly through my sweaty pong and continued agony. My very first clinch with a breast, boom, I wasn't expecting the body to be able to react in that way, there couldn't have been enough blood. I felt thwarted as she drew away with her pretty nose wrinkled up.

When I'd regained my wits and was once again whiff free, we set a date, the first date available, my very first solo date, the following week, which, in school days, is a donkey's age and a half away. We both survived our lessons and continued hanging out in break-times, counting the days, ever more excited that we'd get some privacy to hug, maybe get to nuzzle each other's faces, which we'd started to do a bit, (just rubbing noses though,) maybe we'd get to touch each other's waists and chests and tongues, possibly even more. The mind boggled. Dreams, oh, such dreams; a vibrant flurry of exotic colours.

At this time, cigarettes were found in my sister's bedroom, along with a diary admitting to all kinds; when she'd smoked, who she'd been smoking with, where she hung out and why, who she fancied, what she'd like to do about it, when she might be planning to do things about it, that kind of a thing, and she got grounded for a month.

Not, may I repeat, *not* a way to encourage creative writing.

Arguing with parents on her behalf, against such an unjust punishment for a breach of privacy, perhaps a little over-heatedly, I received two weeks grounding for myself.

This vile circumstance scuppered the first romantic meeting. So be it, that's life, I remained stoic. My excitement doubled, and redoubled exponentially, although she was a bit miffed.

Soon after, she insisted that I should go away with her on a weekend camp she had planned with an adventurous group she was involved with, important to her, sexy times afoot. Yes, yes yes yes yes, please. I'd rarely been so keen to do a thing, also stymied because I remained grounded, despite best efforts.

Tension ratcheted up everywhere as the weekend in question hove into view, arrived, stayed, and passed without nuzzling.

She thought I'd been making excuses because of her braces, I had my suspicions that she'd got together with someone else at the love-weekend away. Either way, paranoid or paranoid, she wouldn't speak to me for the rest of our school days, picking up her stuff and running away whenever I'd approach.

She salted the wounds by getting her friends to tell me that she'd started the rumour herself. I didn't know what to think. Having only nasty words for someone once-loved, is confusing.

Dreams became muddled and ice-cold, the campfire doused, darkness and thick fog filled the glade. Anyone could just walk in. Occasional passing she-devils would taunt, shriek, and cackle from somewhere near in the blackness, just outside of vision.

I fumed and hid in my shell again, and that was that.

8: And God Said, Let There Be Light

So yeah, there was another girl, my sister's friend's sister, whose name I forget. Conversation was hard work and so we sat in stony silence on a cold wall, chain-smoking cigarettes in a biting wind. Unexpectedly, an angry Cuttlefish struggled to suck out my front teeth. When it finally abated, she spoke matter of factly of the great many boys she'd kissed before.

Taken aback, germs filled my mind, I wanted to run off, but, being new to all this, I sat and listened to her life experiences instead, in hope of learning something valuable, for once.

Very quickly I learned that I wanted no knowledge of shared lovers whatsoever in the slightest. Not now, not ever. Thanks.

It was nice that she'd felt special with these other boys, she'd obviously been affected by them, she'd even spent many years and months dating and shagging some of them, but I'd become blood-brothers with those boys, the list of official germ-carriers had begun, we were now all impure, infected with the same bacterial evils through our sharing of her contaminated juices. I tried to make a mental list of these chaps, so I could meet with them and ask about their health, but when it turned into a very long list of names she'd snogged once, just for a bit of fun, I stomped off feeling physically violated.

She had forced her Demon into me when I'd been looking the other way. There wasn't enough mouthwash in the world.

I climbed back into my shell, slammed the lid shut and steamed like a mollusc.

She came round with her noisy sister a few more times to loudly harangue me into hanging out. We didn't get on, at all, and so we didn't hang out.

And that was that was that.

9: And There Was Light

School was out. Life moved on. I got over the germ thing, eventually. Horizons expanded. I gave up my newspaper round, got a first proper job at a 'Scottish' burger-chain for the summer, then immediately took a week off work to play in a jazz band, claiming falsely that I had scarlet fever. Getting a doctor's note was a truly shameful business.

Tertiary College loomed. I'd chosen a tough music course across the county, accessible only by train. Freedom to party beckoned. Offers were on the table, but, all-day burgers first.

Romance with a talented buxom beauty in another town seemed certain. One bright beauty had invaded the dreams suddenly and recklessly. We'd met at various musical gatherings, she'd seemed keen, smelled great, had gravity-defying hair, a beautiful smile, she'd openly declared she wasn't a virgin; all the fuel required to overcome deep-set boyhood reverence. I'd never fallen head over heels in lust at first-sight until then, when, on a promise, my inner bounce bounded back. Boing.

If she wasn't to eat me alive, I had to grow up and toughen up, so I'd made psychological preparations for massive success and enormous failure. The love game had to work out at some point, but if it didn't work out this time, I'd be prepared for the very *very* worst that the world could throw at me. No? No problem.

Days before college began, I learned that she'd started dating the school goalkeeper. I wasn't expecting *that*. It was him who'd told me, while I was at work, not hanging out. Gutted.

He started to invade my dreams, following me about, pissing on my campfire, drawn to my heart's desires to tarnish them, by putting his grubby goalkeeping mitts all over them.

I whistled from the ears, and shrank back into my shell.

10: And on the First Morning Came a Letter

Digitally speaking, I'd quite enough zeros on my scorecard. My one, my 1, my I, my me, myself, the internal id or qi, or whatever, had made a blunt decision; I needed another I, to make two. An I for an I, a truth for a truth; nature's way of setting a balance. You think about me and I'll think about you. Done. Sold, to the shy desperate youth in the shabby shorts.

Angry with malefactors, fed up with being snubbed, I became fixated on finding 'The One', so for a short while, around the end of school, college a bit, I got into the habit of sending letters to favourite girl friends. There had to be a soul-mate who wouldn't be torn from dreamscape at *some* point.

Several girls, at different times, received sudden bursts of messy letters, impetuously scrawled with provocative declarations of flowering loves, affection-inspired creative outpourings of yesteryear, as if Dickens were my only amorous advisement. Overt wishes for reciprocal contact unconcealed in effervescent pictures, cartoons, stories, jokes and one-liners, scribbled in every spare space in tiny writing, unchained thoughts filled the margins, not a single scrap of paper wasted.

A letter is an exciting process. The build up of sending it. The feeling walking up to the box to post it. The pause before you let go. The immediate regret of sending it. The acceptance it has gone.   The waiting and wondering what they'd think. The day when it might possibly not have arrived yet. The day knowing that they *must* have it. The knowing it should've been read by now. The wondering if they are now thinking about you. The waiting for a reply. The reply. The possible writing of another. A wonderful game of connection as generations have seen it, sending good vibes over distance in the best way imaginable.

If one doesn't put what one thinks out there in the world, one won't know if one happens to be barking up the right pole. Screw Valentine cards from guess who; letters have The power of 'know' to heft about mightily. Sign it, date it, be proud of it, I thought. No cloak and dagger nonsense, no pressure to meet, or agree, just speak one's truth comedically, where possible, give passions a voice, and hope there'll be some point of interest that may blossom between sheets somewhere down the line.

But beware, such fervour laid out explicitly for commentary, in hope that a shared discipline makes connection, places one's bollocks bare on the butcher's block for bashing black and blue. My benign babble, like a flibbertigibbet blabbering, with pictures, bore fruit. Blubbing about being unbeddable backfired, badly.

Even with a positive first reply, after the third or fourth had been sent out in quick succession it would be shut down swiftly as I remember. Blooms of unfettered infatuation bursting forth inverted rapidly into a vacuum of loathsome mortification. Rejection will do that to a person. That much is crystal clear.

I became acutely aware of my literary failures as a man-boy when those letters were unpicked by greater intellects than mine. It couldn't be said that any replies were sneering *exactly*, but sneery, sneerish, sneeresque. I should be grateful, I suppose, that I didn't send any more, and grateful to them too, probably, maybe. At the time, though, the very bottom had fallen out of my bottom, which is no pleasant experience for anybody.

For such over-emotion, juvenile ardour and hubristic certainty, these days, even for a legal minor, sexual harassment would probably be the charge, even though I'm convinced the letters weren't overtly sexual, or even, remotely sexual. It felt genuine, but was probably pretty creepy. Thankfully, no thought police, as yet. Regardless, I hope the letters have all been burned and that we'd all laugh about it now in the full light of adulthood.

Moving on.

11: After the Letter Came the Word

Virginity is important, ask anyone. Everyone wishes for their first time to be memorable. As occasions go, for most creatures, it is the sole purpose of life.

It was early '97, I was seventeen, a scruffy longhair, a happy-go-lucky chap. Childhood had been content-rich though worldly-wise-poor, living my cotton-wool life in an idyllic seaside town.

I had fallen very much in love, again. This time, an intelligent, beautiful, talented musician, living in a distant Sussex village. Miraculously, despite my persistent odour, we'd been officially boyfriend and girlfriend for months. It'd taken her a while but, she'd reached goddess status in my dreams; *silver* goddess status. I'd leap out of bed upon waking with the joy of ticklish excitement in every nerve, breathlessly exploding over and over in each new moment, propelled out of the door with joyful heart from the mere contemplation of long happy days flirting. I was going to lose my virginity to this girl. Almost definitely, definitely almost definitely, I could feel that truth in my bones.

She came from a Catholic family, which buggered things up rather. Anticipation is its own reward, I believed, maybe, but oftentimes one desires the damn package to arrive already.

We'd hugged and kissed a bit, just enough to imagine a lifetime of enjoyment. Meaningful knee-squeezing and hand-holding was more of our thing, to save sharing my halitosis. We even got our tops off once or twice when no one was around for a few minutes of frolicking, which was very very *very* exciting, but that was about as far as fleshly touching went. We were both finding our way, setting out what we were comfortable with, and not. Unsure of morality past the midriff, I was more than willing to learn, eversomuch; she, less so.

From a Protestant Creationist Evangelical Church, *my* base level was; puritanical, patriotic, ideological and homophobic, as well as; naïve, confused and sure I was wrong about most things. In the real world, that meant that I was a virgin who collected union flags, thought without thinking, and took the mickey out of boys wearing make up, not cruelly, just a bit offishly. My parents weren't to blame, they were kind and caring to everyone, but the translated scriptures they ascribed to were difficult to interpret lightly in a changing liberated world. I had no idea how the Catholic religion and modern life would've affected her, maybe she'd be a nymphomaniac, I held out youthful hope.

The Catholic Protestant divide wasn't an issue for our parents, quite the reverse. Our town MP had been blown up brutally by Irish militants a few years previously, due to this, or maybe, despite it, the intermingling of all denominational communities was encouraged for the sake of diversity. They were glad of the assumed sanctity we both applied and 'maturity' we showed out there amongst the Heathens. By finding partners already members of His club, if only by birth, they saw it as if we'd hedged our bets with their Godhead, albeit One with regulatory equivalent directives. Besides which, they were happy if we followed our hearts and could make each other smile.

Despite many doubts about most things, I still believed in the inviolability of marriage. One can rarely avoid the sanctity of innocence and purity in discussions of morality. We were virgins, this still seemed to me as the correct way of going about things. Rational or not, hippies on a hillside under a tree or not, patriarchal or feminist or not, God-given or not, Proverbs 22v8, Matthew 19v5-6, Quran 4v34, BoM Jacob 2v27-28, Manusmriti 3v55-56, Raag Aasaa Mehal 1, or not, the process of marriage worked for me and was something I desired. Love between two people forever. Consummation also very much and especially, how extra-super-special two pure virgins coupling would be.

Deferred gratification has a lot to be said for it. Nnnnnngh. Anticipation and denial. Nnnnnngh. We'd cut our paths. Nnnnnngh. We waited. Nnnnnngh. But. Nnnnnngh. Out there. Out *there* somewhere. Somewhere in the big wide world out there lived people whom these overly-specific rules did not apply to. Envious was I of their looser living. Covetously did I lust after my neighbour's ass. It seemed unnatural to be waiting when the feeling for procreation was so strong. Hormones said differently to scripture and I knew that, of the two, these strong impulses were, at the very least, something certain one could believe in.

There being no obvious handbook for such things, I'd long ago made bargains with God to orgasm freely and yet maintain a pathway to heaven. When learning how to orgasm efficiently, the disgrace, borne heavily, took years to clear the system whilst my Guardian Angel voyeurs looked on laughing, but it was worth it. Over time, the angels and I had decided that masturbation wasn't one of the deadly sins, more a celebration of biological life, I just wished they weren't watching. Now I had to convince *her* that it could be mutually beneficial to our lives.

I'd not attended the family church regularly for a few years. There being so many sects, so many religions, why would my tiny community be right? What should God do when someone else, more blessed than I, is praying for a different outcome to my prayer? Chosen people? Answers brought the idea of God-given eugenics into the spotlight rather more than is healthy for an impressionable mind. I was filled with envy, I wanted to be chosen. I truly believed that only Christians and Jews were in contention for an afterlife, and no one else. That didn't seem fair somehow, but those were the rules of the game handed out at birth. My heart had gone out to those following false gospel simply by being born in the wrong place, until, after a while, I'd become aware of the insane brazen pride that required, and started developing those first inklings, that we cannot *all* be right.

Upsetting everyone at every stage, bit by bit, I started to distance myself from family rituals; refusing to say Amen after grace, or grunting, then pointedly thanking the chef in English, that kind of thing. I'd probe my parents over the dinner table on pressing matters; questioning whether sex out of wedlock was evil or natural, if consubstantiation was a cannibalistic ritual, whether God spoke in car bombs, whether the Roman Pope's atonement of paedophile priests was, in fact, a double hypocrisy, whether those priests would enter heaven if they pled for forgiveness, whether that's the sort of Heaven that anyone would want to go to, whether or not the Muslims or Hindus went to a real Heaven like ours, the really tricky stuff. I'm not really sure that I learned very much.

A mixture of zealous Lutheran and mischievous contrarian, false belief offended me as if I was at war. If my own beliefs could be found to be false, as I was, in fact, finding, then I'd be at war with myself until I'd learned cross-cultural living. Miracles seemed contentious; the power of prayer mute. Apparently you need to *really* mean it or it won't work, like children's magic. But what of free will? Can prayer affect another's behaviour?

My very favourite wind-up at the dinner table was to pry innocently into whether or not weather itself could be influenced in one's favour if one prayed hard enough, and what that meant to church events washed out. I'd tease about the small God of car-parking-spaces, I'd heard too many witnesses celebrating God's grace for supplying parking spaces, especially from the church leaders, to ever let that one go. Imagine a desired thing, now wish it true, the power of positive thinking and confirmation bias. Hmmmmm. Really? Adults? *Really?* Much bothered me.

Apostasy bothered me the most. Still does. Unless a child will accept every part of a parent's faith verbatim, prayer and all, the embedded truth of Hell and damnation for leaving the faith is an especially callous self-punishment to be left with.

Part of the inner child wishes the whole package of Heaven and Hell to be true, but whilst one slides from a Holy position, Hell *is* the base assumption. When one desires the dignity of an ethical code without the threat of violent punishment hidden within it, even the softest family bed can be a prison of the mind.

When one becomes aware that one's received a subjective history of the world from the same source as has delivered one's certain scriptural uncertainties, one's own assumptions and data-sets are not to be trusted. If one lacks the reasoning power to differentiate truth from fiction, then one starts to doubt one's very sanity, the sanity of one's family, one's community, the whole world, caught in a perverse societal loop of constraint and requirement that one is singularly powerless to change.

Not wanting to offend anyone adds an extra burden to remain flockbound. As a child, the situation is such that one is immediately confused by the status of religion when mixed up with the history of peoples, politics, genetics, economics and war, all of which one's been given mixed signals about, only *some* of which any one faction is allowed to talk about at any time, and even then, only incompletely. No amount of fractional discussion on the thoughts and actions of an unknowable God can be important to whether what is written down about Him is actually true or not.

With such a tiny portion of truth accessible, one ignores the obvious errors and 'facts' that aren't facts, instead concentrating on the consolations of God's love, mercy, blessings and the hope of an afterlife. All the while feeling utterly wretched about it. Worse still, the healthier a child's natural propensity to trust and respect their elders and community, the worse the contrition. As a gentle soul, rather than assumed joys of our family's hallowed rapture filling daydreams with self-congratulatory privilege, it was instead a natural empathy for those poor souls who'd failed to get into my Heaven who would thrust their way into nightmares through the widening cracks of dreamscape.

Visions of ancestors burning in Hell caused insomniac terrors that would shake me awake with shrieks of sadness and dread. A real, true, genuine belief in Dante's daemonic Hell, in the twentieth century. So afflicted was I that it hijacked daydreams and sat behind the eyelids whenever eye blinked.

Imagine, if you would, demons, currently, continually, inflicting worse-than-anyone-can-even-imagine on human souls. Just imagine that. No, worse than that. And worse than that.

Worse than hot irons scorching ever-replenishing flesh. Worse than being peeled with a blunt knife, rubbed in salt, then fried in battery acid. Worse than being egg-sliced in a bath of lemon juice. Worse than eternal buggeration with a sharpened bassoon. Worse than drowning in shark-infested frogspawn. Worse than feeling all the pain in the universe at once through the teeth. No, worse than that. These things matter. For a child with only basic reasoning skills, complete faith in the family, and an overly-vivid imagination, they really do matter a lot.

At the time, back in '97, for some dumb reason or another, *it* still had *its* claws in me. Either; all of *it's* true, or none of *it's* true, or some of *it's* true. Or, some of *it* is partly true to some people and not others. Whatever. A certain truth is that somebody has been lying to somebody else somewhere along the line, and people, many people, just like myself, were the exact type of angry perplexed idiots being produced as a direct end result.

Ready to break the chains of my pick and mix religion, I desired intelligent communication with the people out there, out *there*, on the outside of the bubble, people who wouldn't allow the childish imagination free reign, I demanded facts.

The anticipations of oncoming freedoms and responsible adulthood filled the heart with all the excitement of a puppy, my best years ahead of me, ready to face the world on my own, get some experience, build a shed, make an impact of assort, any impact would do. Normal stuff for any aspiring youth.

12: After the Word Came the Sentence

Out one evening quite early, I found myself at the town jazz club. Great. I even got in. I'd never hung out as a punter before and was finding myself enjoying the experience immensely.

I was looking for gigs from the club manager. He'd previously seen me play at the venue and I wanted to press him into more of the same. Luck was on my side. Not only did he want to give me gigs, but free drinks too. He was trying out new cocktails, as he put it. I felt honoured. I felt privileged. I felt obliged.

This is going to be a good night, I'll just have one or two, nail down a few gig-dates, watch the start of the band's set when they arrive, then head home for a good sleep and a joy-filled day lost in love tomorrow. What a great plan, I thought.

My girlfriend and I were to meet for lunch the next day. We'd organised a tipsy day together in the sun for consensual testing of how far we could push our less than puritanical ideas of budding romance upon each other. Marvellous things afoot.

Sat at the bar I felt pretty smug. At that particular moment, a genuine young adult, an authentic human being, the pubescent makings of a good man. I cherish the memory of that feeling. Never again would I feel so old.

Memory gets lost in a thick smoky haze of friendly faces and many people buzzing around, a full club, loud live music, carousing and laughter, another drink, another, a comfier seat, plenty of knee-touching, a blurred image of shapes in outline, less shapes and quieter music, then a very slow fade to black.

Waking. Movement. Margarine. Margarine? Odd. Strange dream. Slowly a distant awareness of a feeling of contact, it seemed pleasant enough. Adrift in my nonsensical reverie, in a world of love and gaiety, I floated blissfully back to sleep.

When perception returned once more to my head, there it was again, a whiff of margarine in the warm air and an odd painful feeling I couldn't describe, closer this time, uncomfortably so. My mind moved to a very painful shit I'd had after eating too much corn as a child. An uneasy feeling crept up my spine.

Action, my head said. No, replied the body. I tried to move my head but neck muscles failed to respond. Odd, my body said. I tried my arms but they'd no strength. I buckerooed cerebrally but nothing happened. Oh, good, I'm still in the dream, I hoped.

There was dialogue in the room but it was odd, barely decipherable, the murmur of background characters, wizards making incantations or similar. Words made no sense at all, mere lumps of woolly noise in a drifting world. My sleepy inner-voice dribbled incoherently, language meant nothing.

Lying face down, I could feel a scratchy something on the back of my thighs pinning me down under its weight, but couldn't begin to conceptualise what it could've possibly been.

Time passed between a pleasurable fantasy, dreamy discomfort then abrupt acute dry ripping pain of full sober realisation, suddenly fully aware of exactly what was happening behind me, entirely unable to respond, except possibly to gibber dumbly.

Anoesis in the waking world, stark awareness, a living rag-doll, a mind-prisoner in an inactive body, a mounted trophy head opening its eyes to take in the horror of stuffed actuality.

Hate and loathing filled me up as friction, pain, and the cooling relief of lubricant became my world. Words still failed me, speech was impossible, I could barely think, but the anaesthetic was beginning to wear off and I was waking up to wreak havoc.

Breathing was difficult and nasty with the face buried in dribbly pillows. Still pinned, adrenalin fueled, expending every available effort, I fought, bent, twisted, joggled and wriggled to the edge of the huge bed and hung my head over the side to catch a breath.

Stifling hot air hit me in the face, feculent with the sweaty margarine; a half-scooped tub of: St Ivel's: Gold, sat inches away on the floor, with a tablespoon stuck in it. I retched violently as it became apparent *exactly* why the margarine was there.

Those dawning realisations I shall remember always as the moment I'd become a man. There it was forever in an instant. I knew empirically that I was being, was going to have been, will always have been raped as a virgin. Dribbling onto the floor at bed's edge in an unknown room, unwiped tears and snot pouring down my chin, no limb control, arms tucked somewhere, lungs crushed, pain shooting through hips and back, heaving in the greasy air, helpless, pitiable, desolate, a fleshy plaything.

Not for me; rose petals, candles, long baths, scented oils and nuzzling femininity, as every ounce of being wished for and longed for, oh no, for me instead; the acrid piquancy of vinegary semen, man-sweat, margarine; outrage, anguish, and despair.

I stirred with enough vitality to protest, quietly at first, barely a breath, finding my voice, winding it up, filling my lungs until yawping loudly, a bark from the deepest gut of inner being, as a bull seal defending his territory. A heavy door slammed savagely. The room shook. My head rang. Pangs of pain and sickness hit me in waves. I stopped my protestations; I hadn't even the energy to vomit. Mortality, an easy decision away. Insentience overcame all. Cataclysmic visualisations filled the thumping mind. Timelines spread and stretched in concentric waves around me in phase with my heartbeat. Myriad sets of multiverses ripped from probability with my guardian-angels still trapped inside them, mourning my death. Vibrating bubbles, spheres of profundity, hovered significantly just beyond reach then floated away from my flailing grasp. All futures with inherent self-worth and boundless joys within them vanished from view. Intensely alone and inconsolable, I watched them drift away, then disappear, and mourned their loss, bitterly.

I've heard other people say they've never had a hangover like it, well, I've never had a hangover like it. It didn't feel like any booze hangover I've ever known. And I've *really* gone looking. Of course, I didn't know it then, but it was the drugs. Heavy drugs. Heavier than any since taken in hope of finding some answers.

After what seemed like forever, I'd recovered enough for noises to become words, to become sentences, to become thoughts of possible escape. Bodily control returned enough to move weak limbs a little bit and complain vocally, in recognisable syllables of actual meaning, with sufficient force to compel him to stop.

I clumsily rolled away, got a sheet between us, wrapped it tightly around myself, twisted savagely against the headboard and spent several distressed minutes trying to catch my breath. I looked directly into the eyes of my naked assailant. Oh, it's you, I thought. Cunt, I also remember thinking.

I don't remember falling asleep, but I awoke stripped naked on the bed, the sheet had now been removed. I gradually pulled myself together again, but couldn't remember how to think, and so found the sheet and promptly fell back to sleep.

On and on it went: wake, weakly find sheet, fall asleep, awake, find clothes, partially clothe, collapse, awake naked, find clothes, walk, collapse, walk, fail to turn doorknob, stagger, hit face on doorknob, wake stripped naked on the bed, roll away, grab clothes, collapse, every juddering step a fresh new hell, brain exploding, walls wobbling, ears awash, blurry vision, *finally* deal with door knob, leave room, oxygen, cool oxygen, fill lungs, fill lungs again, corridor, clothe, run, stumble, run.

Down down down three stories of steep unforgiving stairs, much on the seat of my ruined fundament, to the front door; the only exit, locked and bolted, with extra locks and bolts.

After much muddled miserable contemplation in the stairwell, I realised that I'd lost my wallet.

Anguish asphyxiated me in pulsating waves.

Choices were limited. Keys were required to leave. I climbed with some pained difficulty back up up up to the bedroom above the club. I confronted him, incensed by what had happened. But I was a mess, bawling hysterically, he was never going to let me run out into the street in that state loudly proclaiming his evil ways. I wailed and gnashed my teeth and threatened to smash stuff unless he let me out of the front door. Now. Now...

He smoothed my aggression with a bit of his own. I flinched and fell with my back against the wall, slid, sat and smouldered. He calmed my fury, for, until I'd be civil, I was still his to toy with. He asked me to find a happy space, I thought of my girlfriend and wailed like a toddler.

I was late. Very late. My beloved girlfriend already halfway across the county waiting. He offered me a lift. My flood of tears stopped just long enough to accept. He insisted that I laugh a genuine laugh before he'd give access to the keys. The process entirely vexing; compliance, the only escape. He asked me to dress properly. I smartened up externally, dried my tears, smiled my required smile, forced some air through the throat and sat calmly as if the shaking body wasn't sobbing at all, until the next flood pouring over the cheeks ruined the charade and started the process over. There was no option to any of it.

Ultimately we were talking like adults again. We looked for my wallet without success, then, finally, left the building. Less than an hour later, we were parked in a lay-by, he wouldn't drive another metre unless I'd suck his cock right there in his car.

By this point I was broken. Deeply profoundly sullen, to put it mildly. Filled with self-hatred, a head full of slimy serpentine words, nothing in the pockets, no transport, no escape, still recovering from whatever it was in the system, a long walk from anywhere, his sweaty manicured hand in my hair, soothing encouraging whispers in my ears; worthless meat in a scrap-heap universe.

Reviled and disgusted, stinky slug met tongue and trepidation. It went against everything I'd ever stood for as a God-fearing homophobe. How I detested men and their evil ways. It was as if the anthropomorph of militant feminism itself had taken its dick and shoved it down my throat. Not to say the interaction was a success, far from it. I couldn't stop myself from contact gagging, he subdued quickly with all the retching, I turned on the verbals, refused to continue, and, all in all, it didn't last long.

He dropped me off at the wrong place on the edge of town, irritated with me that I wouldn't put out properly. I wished him death as I watched his car disappear through a blur of frenzied tears, I prayed for divine vengeance, *expecting* his car to crash, spitting his taste meaningfully until he was out of sight. I cursed myself for not punching him in it or biting the thing clean off. I imagined sweet retribution, armed with a spiked battering mace.

Distraught and enfeebled, I raced across town with a pronounced limp in both legs. Arriving at the meeting spot, I searched desperately, but my girlfriend had already gone home. No mobile phones back then, of course, so I passed a while waiting. Mainly standing. I begged some money off a stranger and called her landline. Her parents weren't happy with me. She too wasn't best pleased. I decided to walk to her house, several miles up the big hill. Less than halfway up, I stopped at a bench. Realisation dawned that I wasn't going to make it. I rested. Downhill footsteps juddered in my fragile swaying state. I found another bench. I rested. By and by, I decided to go home and had to jump the train to do so.

So that was that. Life moved on. Silence was maintained. My girlfriend eventually forgave me. Her father gave me a good dressing down about respect. I didn't deal with any of it very well, tearing away and shaving my head. The hair grew back a bit and she forgave me again. Hollow rotten snivelling aplenty, but I wasn't dead, so that remained its own glorious reward.

13: And the Sentence was Read

There are worse things than rape. A lot worse. Worse than that too. It's a terrible shitty world. I hadn't lost a wife, or dog, or been kicked out of a house, or been disowned by my kids, or thrown out of a homeland to starve, or had a family bombed to death in a war that I didn't want to fight. I wasn't a dung-beetle, or plankton, nor a zillion worse things, and I was free.

I counted my blessings. I had a loving family, I still had all my limbs and senses, a comprehensive education at my back, I could work on my wits; it seemed comparatively insignificant in the grand scheme of things, just another anomalous statistic.

Truly, it seems petty to bemoan one's lot once one is free in a free world to make one's own choices in life. I've always considered myself lucky that this is the worst that can be dredged up, on balance though, I wasn't feeling *overly* blessed.

In 1997, if you'd had a homosexual experience you weren't allowed to give blood, nicely demonstrating the cultural stigma attached to such an act even in *late* twentieth century Britain. I wasn't being chemically castrated or imprisoned like some previously famous examples, but, all the same, I felt a fool fending off forthright phlebotomists with fluffy falsehoods.

While maintaining a Zen-like exterior, or so I thought, internal monologues became insufferable, maintaining and sustaining an odious inner victimhood. Positive emotions no longer arrived when whistled for. Dreary in company, manic with friends, in the first instant alone, resentment and loss, seriousness and overthinking where the euphoria of impulsive burgeoning youth should have been partying. Even the joys of masturbation were sacrificed to the impending sense of being shot through the heart with a heavy-cannon at close range.

At the time, self-proclaimed victimhood was frowned upon. We still had WW2 veterans in the community, they'd known the WW1 veterans, going back generationally into true barbarism, the stiff upper lip was prevalent in our corner of the world. Chin up and all that, maintain the belief that victims are *only* women, or foreign, or dead, and all that, keep a respectful silence of personal effrontery, what what, roll with it, there's a good chap, if you really wouldn't mind too awfully.

I kept it all secret from my family. There were many reasons. Not least because I assumed they'd want the only jazz club in town closed down, which wasn't going to happen because of me, no effing way. To get to gigs, with large amplifier and double-bass, a parent or other would drop me off and pick me up at great expense to their sleep patterns, just to know I'd be safe. They, being teachers, needed their wits and sleep to do their jobs, live their lives, and stay cool; I didn't want to burden them further. In my own sweet way I was protecting them from more stress, after all; a problem shared *is* a problem doubled.

Mentally, I stewed in confusion, uncontrollable dry-retching became normal. Cranial visions nauseated the gut and weakened the gag reflex, an exhausting routine. Bulimia an easy choice. Teeth and tongue cleaning a pained rarity. It would have been difficult to say that my hygiene had been directly affected, it would have been difficult to tell, but it certainly didn't improve.

A mountain of learning and upheaval lay ahead, but, I couldn't feel sorry for myself, I was a free man in a free world. That's the joy of peacetime pessimism; base privilege. Freedom itself is the ultimate consolation. I kept my hatred on a short leash, every day it appeared like whack-a-mole, a never-ending series of things to pour scorn upon. Death felt like a good option to remove the pain quickly, but somehow all a bit too sudden. A pusillanimous pussy, I made a choice to smoke and drink lethally instead. A coward's choice. A thinking man's suicide.

For a short unsustainable period I became a bit of a tearaway, losing a lot of would-be friends while doing stupid things; foolish things, out for attention things, look at me acting unthinkingly things, listen to what I think things, I don't care if any approve of acting crazy things, stopping is not an option so go away and shuddup things. Bridges burned, never to be rebuilt.

A few close friends worked out that things weren't altogether perfectly okay, when they found me in the college common-room inscribing the popular catchword of the moment in neat, inch-high lettering onto my forearm with a pair of compasses. Never forget, it screamed in scarred flesh, never *ever* forget.

The self-destruction stopped at the very same moment that I crashed and wrote off the family car, drunk, with friends on board, two weeks after passing my driving test, at the same time that parents were taking a first brief well-deserved holiday, having thought me to be responsible for my actions, mistakenly. I wasn't proud, unable to breathe with the wretchedness of it.

Humility thrust from every angle, however, reconciliation seemed a long way off. Sure, the parents were glad we'd survived and that death was avoided, but the never-ending paperwork for the authorities was an unwanted task that none enjoyed. False claims had been added to the list of insurance pay-outs, only I *knew*, but no one was on-side to fight that cause with me.

The magistrate date had been set for the end of the summer, grudging self-pity grew, expanding into every available hour. The head imploded daily with vacuous family/friend double-think, lost in what it was possible to say and to whom. Levels of respect were due to loved ones, but frustration grew that this impasse didn't, perhaps *couldn't*, stretch to a serious discussion of what constitutes right and wrong. Not that I'd've been able to have that debate with a brain starved of rationality. I kept my victimhood hidden under my hat, long sleeves over my scars, and hobnailed walloping cudgel in the cupboard.

14: And the Sentence Continued

Another great memory I'd like to share comes from around the same time, before I'd achieved any financial independence, or basic knowledge of people, etc.. I had been out in the world actively pursuing leads, running about in custody of a double-bass, gaining some *extra* extra-curricular musical experience.

A soon-to-be-retired schoolmaster ran an amateur orchestra locally, bolstered by teenage talent coming through the county schooling system, of which I was, at the time, a part. Nearly four times my age, he took a shine to me. I mean, who wouldn't? Right? I was becoming a fine young specimen. *I* would've.

No one noticed what was happening in all the jolly goodwill. With all of the altruism and putting oneself out of one's way for others, the currency on which the whole amateur music community is based, it is easy to miss just one kindness too far. The grooming, for that's what it was, happened over months and years, involving regular gifts of chocolates and flowers to my mother. He took on transportation of the bass to rehearsals, a win-win for the folks. For me; responsibility and respect, name-checks in concerts, exposure to knowledgeable interesting people, and chances to get musical experience. He played on and preyed upon my teenage desperation for any standard of musical opportunity and desire for immediate recognition.

After a short and intensive working period for some concert, he started to proffer sleepover evenings at his house along the coast, a reward for having made extra efforts in getting other contemporaries involved. Roast dinner, my favourite. He'd asked, I'd told him, he'd offered roast. And, quietly, wine. And, as far as everyone was concerned, myself included, and extra-especially, a separate bed in a separate room.

He was a fair composer, a public-schoolmaster, an upstanding member of society and professed to be a Christian, on paper, it *should* all have been fine. Sleepover was agreed with the family because he lived a distance away and I didn't particularly object too much, after all, I wanted to get drunk on the wine he'd promised without facing my parents hungover. Being poor, underage, and experience poor too, I actually wanted to go the *first* time.

In reality it led up to intensely difficult situations I was patently not ready for, involving romantic dinners with candles, booze, music and, *yes*, intelligent conversation, which was totally fine, but as awkward as one might expect with an age gap of nearly fifty years. Wine was guzzled, piano was played, songs were sung, hoorah the lads. Second bottle, third bottle, fourth.

Suddenly, onscreen was the first hardcore porn I'd ever seen. It did things to me that I remember fondly and I sat transfixed. I was faintly surprised that he had such things on his tellybox given his social standing, but he was single and free and wow-wow I can see why. However, open wanking was a definite shock for me. My own penis remained sheathed. He told me not to be so sheepish for this is what all the boys at public-school do. Meanwhile, I, a puritanical virgin who'd attended a state comprehensive, sat there embarrassed, wide-eyed, disgusted, repulsed, horny and confused. I drank my wine and found more.

Later on still, upstairs. Oh, you always brush your teeth naked do you? Oh, the spare room has chairs on the bed does it? Oh, so there's a spare bed made up in *your* room, you say? Oh, so these beds have been bolted together, you say? Oh.

Nakedness was his thing. It wasn't really my thing. Not with him, certainly. It still isn't a favourite pastime. Cerebral recoil I attach to that bloated gout ridden body of his, still inclines me to leave my shirt on for fear of similar judgement from others. He was fascinating, sure, I could allow that he was a nice chap, but the very idea of physical interaction twisted my intestine.

I lay in bed still clothed in shorts and tee-shirt with the duvet pulled up to my chin. Massage? No thanks. Grumpy muttermurmermumbling about ungrateful bloody people. Oh, okay, just a short one, just shoulders though. It'll be better without this duvet here. No it won't. Yes it will. I'd rather not. It'd be better without these clothes. No it wouldn't. Take these off. No. And on it would go, until eventually, after much anguish, his shrivelled wrinkly hirsute flaccidity sat upon my upper buttocks like a bag of Babybels. The stinking clammy pickle would rub up and down my lower spine as he'd expound upon the glories of naked massage, while I'd cry into the pillow and pretend to be somewhere else. A sigh would escape him as his gut landed, a large water-filled balloon rolling up my back. Now it's your turn, here's the oil.

Revolted, guilt-ridden, drunk and exhausted, I'd sit perched atop his swollen back, straddled, going for height, failing not to touch him with my own, prodding and poking at his taut, inflated, pockmarked, greasy, spotty, tough and aged flesh with my painful blistered fingertips.

I didn't understand why this sweaty, liver-spotted, mottled, short, fat, bristly old man was the only companionship a tall slender youth such as I could bag. I wondered why the Lord God Almighty Himself kept offering up such vulgar alternatives to true love, while specifically tormenting me with friends who had found carnal desire to be beneficial to their 'normal' lives.

When energies had been spent, or my cold shoulder finally proven too much for his incessant badgering, he'd land on the pillow and be asleep immediately. I would stare out of the window at the brickwork and dodgy roofing, lost in loops of thought, distracting myself from uncontrollable streams of tears with slapdash philosophy clouded by the mind-forged mania of sin, until the dawning hangover would shut glassy-eyes, so as to enter the bloodthirsty arena of cascading dreamscape chases.

In the morning, I had no idea what to say. He'd just continue with luxury life jovially, and I'd partake until it was time to go. Life cycled on through the red traffic-light without looking.

His advances continued, I blindly allowed it. More flowers arrived for my mum. Each successive time, to protect myself, I'd add to the rules of engagement before agreeing to go back. While acquiescing to plan requests, on the nights in question he'd introduce new nonsense, worming his way around earnest stipulations with more wine and more exciting pornography.

The last time I visited him he'd started composing a double-bass piece, a beautifully hand-drafted manuscript dedicated to me. It was to be a two-movement piece, one for each of my initials: T&F. He'd written the: *Toccata*, and he promised me a: *Fugue*.

Yeah, quite. He was obviously frustrated. Yet, forgivably, it is altogether too clever a piece of punnery to be chastised too heavily, it must have taken him many hours of legwork.

That said; I was deeply concerned at the openness of his implication. We discussed possible options for my middle-initial as a matter of some urgency over dinner that evening.

He invited me to move to Spain with him. I choked on gravy. After this unmistakable revelation, I never ever went back and stopped answering his phone-calls, even rudely hanging-up on him and pulling out the cord, as one could do in those days.

I didn't know what I was getting into.

I wasn't aware.

I wasn't informed.

I didn't want it haunting me.

I didn't want to be thinking about it.

He had no right.

He had no right at all.

Get out of my head, you bastard.

Please, please, get out of my head.

15: And the Sentence Came to a Full Stop

If I am to survive living with the experience of this, I thought, I'd just have to grasp that there are things I don't know about yet. Live through it, or not, go wild, or not, feel hatred, or love, or not. Maybe I needed to show more understanding. There are worse things than being given food, drink and a warm bed.

In better states of mind, my memory is of a lonely individual in his dotage trying to share his love by realising his best intention. My memories are quite clear, in so far as that he was perfectly civilised and a joy to talk with, his enthusiasm when sharing his knowledge of obscure British composers was a credit to his many *many* years dedicated to teaching.

It must be empathically adjudged that: what he'd wanted, was: for the object of his desire, me: to share in the giving of his proffered love, in the forms that that would take: his flirtations. Sound familiar anyone? Everyone?

How easy to be misunderstood by another when realms of acceptability barely overlap within interacting minds. How easy to judge a small drunken manipulation for selfish means as unacceptable, when one might quite like that oneself, if things were different, if power had shifted in another way. I didn't know, I'd personally never had power over anyone, from being a teen, and all that. Never having had sex, *in a loving relationship*, felt as though the world had set out to test me, only me, specifically.

Who is to say what is acceptable? Society? Maybe not. God? Which One? Not mine. Not any one God to have revealed Themself unto me, or whose intentions can be deciphered from a book without the need of an interpretation from those who claim to be blessed with that gift, given by He, She, Him or Herself, the Lord or Lady God, speaking through peasant, or trillionaire.

People are different, paths are long and empathy is a science. If I'd understood what he wanted from our congregation before, it wouldn't have happened, the situation would not have arisen as it would've been thrashed out with stern words beforehand and I would never have gone over in the first place. But then, if I'd understood before, and I'd been more amenable, say, maybe if I hadn't been an unthinking homophobe, or, say, had been a trainee masseur, *then* I may have left such experience without the frightful repugnance branded onto my heart, after all, though nearly fifty years my senior, he was kind and nice, and gentle and loving, which is much more than can be said for many *many* people. It stops the internal wince slightly, soothes it.

Is it Stockholm syndrome? Had I forgiven him his trespass against me? Maybe. Accepted his trespass? Yes. Convinced myself his trespasses weren't trespasses? No, not reliably, no.

In the pursuit of working out the rules to how the game of life gets played, being bruised emotionally is a lot better than being literally bum-raped. Infinitely better. There is no comparison. After all, he hadn't put anything inside me other than a hot meal and several gallons of good wine. I had to check my revulsions, I was no victim, westernised men are fine with homosexuality, it's a legal requirement, if I could just convince myself that it was normal behaviour for me too, *then* memory wouldn't be so reviled, but, unhappily, revulsions they inevitably remained.

I couldn't tell my family about this guy either, it would've caused too much hassle. They'd only tell the police and that would ruin all our lives. I knew from having seen it in the newspapers that the police didn't have a good track record for such things. It was only my word against his, no use in court. Besides which, I justified, he hadn't invaded me as the club-owner had done, there was no hard penis rubbing inside a tube made of my flesh, no soreness, they'd probably not take seriously such a story, of a mere soft phallus tickling the skin, from a hippy long-hair.

Even if the police *were* effective, no one wanted to see nice old men who misguidedly act on their impulses to be hounded and put in jail for the rest of their lives. Or, quite apparently, now, they do, but *back then* the only options available involved a media circus of shame for the victim that I wanted no part of. I felt shame enough already, I didn't want to display my victimhood to any who would judge me, I desired only the freedom to act upon impulse and choose my own destiny.

The aptly named fugue-state softened daily thinking, like an electric carving knife tied to a drill to tackle a particularly stubborn floater, an overload of conflicting neural activity clogged the processors and prevented me from exacting personalised vendetta justice with a blunt-nosed bludgeoning paddle. Oh, how I wished it. I wanted to take out his shins with a chainsaw piece by piece. Vengeance of the painful kind seemed to be a simpler option than to oust him to his peers and the justice of the law, such as it was, but still I couldn't do it, nor could I ruin his planned retirement to his Spanish Villa, because, with the media circus being what it was, no one walked away untainted, and, frankly, I was greatly relieved that he'd be in a foreign country, away from me, the further the better. The hippy inside won the day. Let that shit go, man, let that shit go.

Bring back the stocks says aggrieved I, for aggrieved I would've surely ousted him if that were to be his punishment. Jail-terms and ending a glossy future is too much retribution for a daft drunk old sod whom loved too much. He deserved no better or worse than to have rotten fruit and veg thrown at his head. Vegetable justice. Fairly vengeful, but not life-threatening.

Life-cycles cycled by. Over time, and with distance, I judged it to be a fairly harmless experience in comparison. Not great, not something to my taste, not something I'd encourage the generations to repeat, but a lived experience, which must be, and can only be, dealt with by making efforts to comprehend.

16: And the Sentence was Read Again

For a while I had to retrain the brain from distrusting everyone new if they seemed nice, smiled caringly, or behaved in a friendly manner. It seemed rather a defeat of a free society that a smile or generosity was a trigger for suspicion, but that type of paranoia was a very real issue for a while. People that wouldn't give me time of day I had a natural sympathy for.

Alcohol softened the sadness but let loose a feral animal. One morning, after the lads had a drunken get together at a friend's house, woes remaining as yet unrevealed, we awoke with hangovers and were set to walk the few miles into town. Before we did, we tidied up, collected the leftover drinks, red and white wine, poured it all into one pint glass, to the top, and I necked it. That is exactly where I was at.

On the way into town I became a destructive wobbly mess, making my mark on plants, smashing tiles and generally being a monkey. I got the fear, I felt remorse, I wasn't like this. Okay, happy thoughts; beer in the park, that's happy. The others left me at the edge of town, sensibly. I was going to visit my girlfriend at work, jusht to shay *hell*ow. The others advised against it, but off I went with a spring in my teetering step, quite oblivious.

Turning up at the superstore where she worked, I headed to the beer aisle, picked a selection then headed to her till, grinning. Her reaction was not what I'd expected, no smiles, she didn't even pretend to be pleased to see me, very much the opposite.

I left, upset, refusing to accept how microscopically tiny I felt, inflating myself up, as no one else seemed willing to do it. Screw it, screw this, screw bad vibes, *I'm* going to the park.

On the way, I got caught short, ran behind a nearby bush, but, too late, filled my underpants with the inside of my back.

Off came the shorts and the pants, back on went the shorts. It was on my shoes, and my socks, and my tee shirt, and my jumper, and smeared down my legs. I used all the grass available, dandelion leaves, dock leaves, bush leaves, the carrier bag; I stashed the beers behind the tree, put my pants in the bag and threw them in a bin as I climbed the tall hill to the pub, wiping my shit-stained hands on anything clean as I went.

At the pub, I found the loo and locked myself in it, using toilet paper and the bowl water to scrub off the worst. I remained in there for a while, polluted bog-water running into my socks.

Eventually, I reappeared and asked for, but was refused, a drink. You stink of shit, mate. It was true.

I went outside and met a chap I vaguely knew. Hello, do you want a drink? I'm not allowed one. Oh, I'll get you one. We sat away from other patrons; he told me he couldn't smell anything, but *I* could, and I did my best to clean up whenever possible.

We sat and chatted for hours. Strangely, he was the first person I told of my experiences in any aspect of detail, telling him about the difficulty I'd been having, in not being able to tell anyone about a thing that was tricky to mention. Oblique stuff. I've got a friend who dot dot dot, dash dash dash, dot dot dot, kind of stuff. Then, at a particular low point, I spoke the legend; I think my problem is that I hate all gay men.

He told me that he was gay. I burst into tears. He said it was alright, he wasn't actually gay, just gay friendly, but there was a lot of it about, so I should keep my voice down. Even in my drunken state, I knew he was right, this world does not take kindly to angry sweeping statements of anti-communal opinion.

I opened up to him furiously about all the recent goings on. He told me again that everything was okay, touched my arm, I flinched away violently and made a mad face. He sat with me patiently, until I'd calmed and come to terms with the fact that: it was my *delusion* that every gay man was out to harm me.

He bought us another round of drinks, then a couple more. Conversation continued, brightened, spirits lifted the spirits and we watched the world from our browning patch of grass. As the day turned to dusk, I thanked him for pulling me back from the edge, apologised for the blubbery baboonish babble, apologised for my aggression, apologised for my sadness, apologised for my smell, apologised for not buying a drink, and left him to it. We never met again.

Sensibly, I went to the loo, insensibly, I went to the tree, but the beers had gone, which, although annoying, was probably for the best. Out of good options, I trudged to the train station, got on a train, and fell deep asleep humming of wet cowpats.

Zzzzzz.

Hours later, I awoke alone in an empty carriage as the train pulled into Clapham Junction, heading in the wrong direction.

I jumped out of the train, for, although I'd got onto the correct train going the right way, I'd slept through my stop, slept onwards to the end of the line, slept back to my stop, slept back through the town I'd been drinking in and onwards to London, without a valid ticket, or even, the fare. Cold, very cold, all the windows had been opened and I'd been allowed to sleep on in my own funk, but the chill had gotten into the bones. I shivered with hypothermia, airing on the wind-swept platform.

Another few hours of drunken adventures, to get the late train, without getting thrown-off by an over-zealous ticket-inspector, and, after traipsing a particularly circuitous path home, directly away from other people whenever they appeared, I collapsed in a heap of limbs under a hot shower with a lot to think about.

The very next day the healing process started. Slowly, very *very* slowly; warily, the difficult process of trusting strangers started again. There isn't really a choice. Gradually, very very *very* gradually, and certainly no quicker than that; reticently, the public became kind in the paranoid mind once more.

.

17: And Again

One summer night, hitchhiking home from Hastings after playing bass in a waltzy Sondheim show that ran over, which then, in turn, made me miss the last train; halfway home, the kindly driver put his hand on my upper thigh and asked me if I would be his for the *whole* night. In utter panic, and a flurry of limb-twitching, I flung myself from his car onto a grass verge at speed, rolling to an untidy stop next to a public bin. As I lay there bleeding, staring into the infinity of yellowed lamp-lit sky, I concluded that everyone was, in fact, at it.

I'd come to terms that not *everyone* was a badly-behaved man, yet there were plenty, letting us all down. If *this* was free will, where was the choice? Where was the God-given freedom we're told to be so grateful for? Was the Devil a real force in the world? Was *this* Hell? A Job for life? Was the universe trying to fill a vacuum left by my lack of primal action? Was God Himself gay? Had no one explained to my guardian angels that *I'm not*?

All parameters for a happy life were set in the wrong places. I could not understand why my community had been constructed so as to criminalise the loving of a girl long-desired. Then *this*. Sex out of wedlock is a mortal sin. Ask anyone. If I *were* gay, then I *might've* been happier; I wished that I were, but I wasn't.

Another few miles down the road, another bloke picked me up, before getting into his car, I explained what had happened, and what behaviour I now expected. He must have thought me very *very* rude, but, true to his word, he took me most of the way and remained polite as I relayed the recent events frenetically.

The following week, the County Magistrate emptied my bank account into the national coffers for my drunken transgression. The next day after that, I was off to university.

University of Love
part 1

UNIVERSITY OF LOVE   pt. 1

Prologue: Home Is Where the Heart Isn't

My girlfriend had turned eighteen a couple of days before me, I'd gone over the top on gifts; painting a violin in the union flag, spending all my money on a bunch of crap she really didn't want, boxes within boxes within boxes, lots of crêpe paper. Expensive chocolates for her folks, wrapped by the shop with fancy ribbons of purple and orange.   When challenged by her father for being overtly political, I gawped in dumbfounded amazement.

On the eve of *my* eighteenth birthday, I captained a team to world-championship glory in a local Sussex game: Toads. At the stroke of midnight, the landlord, on our team, invited me to leap across the bar to pull my first legal pint, my tenth of the evening.

The next day, with my first legal hangover, I voted against the Tories in *the* landslide election of a generation. You're welcome.

That same week, girlfriend and girlfriend's friends organised a combined party between a bunch of us, camping in a country garden field with a swimming pool. I thought we might have sex, but no. A surprise cake, made into the shape of a pair of shorts remains the highlight. Sadly, I'd not been able to enjoy any of it through an alcohol-fueled flush of fuck-it.

Saddened and maddened by every single little bloody thing, *including* friends, for sanity's sake, false jollity consumed me. False *fricking* jollity; forced fun, nauseating plastic insincerity with jazz hands, woohoo, six hour's tricky conversation ignored, lost in hurt, faking it to breaking point, hiding floods of tears, laughing fart oo loudly hah as memory skewers stab the ears, grimacing under thunder, corrupt connection, set to broadcast old comedy repeats, befuddling firmly to refuse unwanted care, lacking the skill to course-correct conversation's inexorable pull toward the black hole of an unspoken lie.

Are you alright? *Uh?* Are you alright? *What?* You just phased out there. *Oh,* I'm fine thanks. Are you sure? Ahahahahaha, yeah I'm good, cheers, ahahahahahem. Really? Haha, yep, absolutely fine, thank you, ahahahahem. Is something wrong? Hahahaha, no, ahahaha. Okay, well, if you're sure. Haha, certain, thanks, hehehe, isn't weather great? Well, yeah, quite, in fact, I *just* asked why you won't take your tee-shirt off, it's so hot and everyone else is naked, and *you* jumped in with all your clothes on, so, hello, *hellowo*, you there? *Uh?* Are you alright? *What?* You just phased out, oh, you're a dick. Ahahahahahaha? No, you're a dick.

A youth orchestra tour next up, boys and girls to play away. First day abroad, wallet lost. Slit emotionally; throat to anus, turned inside out doing nasty things for bet money, or beer. Thirsty days, long warm evenings, scrounging any dreg. On the last night, overwrought, 'alcohol poisoning' ensued, having a fit in a foreign ambulance, electrical sensors over my bare torso.

Home. Driving test passed, *soberly* did I ferry myself to and fro, for a fab fortnight, finding far-flung friends in the family Fiat. Parents away, one bad choice; to drive drunk, or to sleep outside. I crashed, badly. Goodbye Fiat, farewell newfound freedoms. Hello remorse, guilt, penitence, and apology. And punishment. Grounded: no booze, no fun, oh, and also, no girls. I didn't mind *that* much, what ground away most of all was being allowed out.

So, I saw cuntychops again, working for *him* at *his* jazz club; he'd phoned on the landline as parents hovered, offering a place in the house band for some guest boogie-woogie piano-shakers on half-a-dozen late-night high-energy shows over the summer; too numb to react, too stupefied to shout, taciturn, I agreed. Within the terrible shadow world of silence, I felt he owed me a courtesy or two and gigs *were* my favoured currency. Absurd as it may seem, I was *grateful* to him for the opportunity. Moderately grateful. I wasn't happy though, oh no, feverishly fucking furious was I, incandescent with eye-popping lividity.

Distrustful of drinks, watching every drop of liquid from tap to lip, I'd ask for a different glass, no, not that one, *that* one, down the freshly poured pints, and then play until my fingers were in tatters, not wanting to unclench the face or delay playing for a single moment, in case I'd inadvertently catch his eye.

The familiar smoky room, long and thin, tucked in, double-bass behind the grand-piano, in front of the drum-kit. So many bad memories, and yet, not quite enough to have me running out screaming, as I was ready to do. I'd planned my escape, where to put my instrument, off stage, how I'd hit him with an uppercut and then wrestle him to the ground and smash his fucking face in until I could smash no more, then run, fly down the stairwell feet first at any who got in my way, out that door, that *damned* door.

Will you be staying for a lock in? No bloody way am I staying for a lock in thank you very much, there's no way I'm having that door locked with me this side of it, *ever* again. Sorry, what? *Uh?*

Music passed in a physical assault on the senses, all new, mostly simple, nothing too hard. Blues in C, and-a-one two three. Brain pain allaying much actual pain, by gig's end, on the right hand, blood-blisters would distend the index and middle fingers from the tips behind the nails, down all three segments of flesh, puffing up across the knuckles, over the metacarpophalangeal join onto the top of the palm, the inside of the thumb, and ring-finger tip too. Bad news when blisters burst mid-gig. Very bad. Messy. Pussy. Bloody. Slippery. Soft layers removed, scooped out, never to be seen again. Kept playing though, that's the job.

The left had cramping and contact issues of its own, index, middle and pinky, bruised and bent, rheumatoid arthritis pending. In hindsight, for a troubled mind under duress, beating and clamping swollen knuckles repeatedly against solid ebony, grating exposed fingertip nerve endings across high-tension wire at 200bpm, was blessed distraction from an inability to breathe with highly-concentrated hatred bubbling away in the lungs.

The last such hateful boogie-woogie gig was for some musical MPs after conference. Television Whoever, came with cameras. The following day, footage appeared on the local news for a few seconds or more, my poor hardworking fingers mostly obscured by subtitle headline text, but there it stood, undeniably, success, the well-honed image of my younger self, wearing shades and funking out in a jazz club, transmitted forever across the galaxy. Cool. I'm cool. The furthest horizon reached, the last tick box ticked, as a teen. Hurrah! Proof captured, stored for evermore on a lost VHS tape.

Being on TV was a big thing back then, much as it is now, perhaps even more so, exactly the kind of thing a lad with my aspiration should have wanted; *had* wanted. Inside, nothing, breathless, a small wholly hollow triumph. Familial elations witnessed with no satisfaction. Overly-affectionate squeals from watching the boy-man-pet doing energetic things with a double-bass, once my very reason to show off and needle for their attention, sat as a blank dullness in a clay mind. Their open pride and joy, which should've prompted grinning, brought interminable glumness and, ultimately, at least on the face of it, a selfish grumpy teenage arsehole. Where love should've been lay a surly sullen sunken void, no pretence to be remotely grateful; wallowing happily, unhappy in the sharp biting wash of self-pity.

The family remained unaware of the manager's transgression. One day, maybe, but not yet, we had religious truth's truth to tackle first. Between us, many words were already insults, many *many* words, so *very* many words that it was slow work to get conversation to where we were able to say anything much at all. Interference sat on the line such that communications had been severed, mere static noise with the volume up. Taking their hardcore material sacrifices for granted, I couldn't help but be deeply upset that they wouldn't stop praying for me, certain proof of prayer's futility kept *fairly* well hidden from them. Ahahaha.

UNIVERSITY OF LOVE   pt.1

UNIVERSITY OF LOVE pt.1

part 1

—

Groan Up

UNIVERSITY OF LOVE pt.1

1: Further Education

When it was time to leave Sussex, I was very happy to go, monocultural boy hits multicultural fan, splat; with childhood's restraints unlocked, stony reality of self-determination dawning, I grew up blinkingly fast with a lot to think about. Don't we all?

A vibey Yorkshire Music College had accepted me, and *I, them*, sure, I'd 'classical' offers from 'good' London Colleges, (double-bass, easy,) but, they'd just not seemed quite far enough away. Life itself would only last a year, or less, definitely, definitely definitely; I just knew. No imagined future, no career planned, no aspiration for a proper qualification, so, I chose to 'study' jazz.

Enthusiastic, but no prodigy, as a classically trained double-bassist, jazz excited me. Unknown order within chaos, and vice versa. Joining now with now, bass thumping time, all the time.

I *loved* jazz. Jazz meant playing. I *loved* playing. Playing turned off the world. Click. Swim. Click. Laughter and applause.

Classical music, however, for a bull-fiddler, passes slowly contemplating the navel, counting multi-rests, waiting to play, two, three, four, forty-one, two, three, four. In stuffy rooms, earnest conductors working on difficult sections with the violins, brass and woodwind, and percussion, on tacet bass sections, filled the long hot summer afternoons of youth with a deep and profound resentment. In my idyllic abyss, visions of life passing without action and distraction were simply insufferable, so, self-indulgently and for lack of better options: jazz. Far away jazz.

Academically, despite best efforts to sabotage exams with alcoholism, required grades had been scraped to the letter, so I qualified, just, by age and poor results, for the last year of state-subsidised degree-level tutelage in England, in Yorkshire, in *jazz*. Hah! Fools. Destiny was on my side. Death would be joyous.

The parents had kindly agreed to stump up for rent until schooling finished, so, for lodgings I moved directly into a house; a large rotten ramshackle terraced house of six people, three boys, three girls. I was going to die in this house, it had been decided.

My ground-floor bedroom sash window, with rusty iron bars on the outside, had been painted shut, with two panes broken when I'd arrived. Some helpful person had inexpertly taped cardboard over it, blocking out much of the natural light, yet still letting in much of the cold. With no practical ventilation, except the door into the hallway to the kitchen, the smell of rot was only overpowered by burnt toast, ashtrays and unshowered teenager. It mattered not, I didn't care, no one I loved would ever see it.

One of the new housemates was a music friend from Sussex who'd been in the family Fiat when I'd crashed it, drunk, through fifteen metres of chain-link fencing, and a telegraph pole, in a naïvely careless risk to our mortality. He never let me forget, just him and his face. Indignity stunned me speechless. He knew stuff, I knew that he knew stuff, he knew that I knew he knew stuff, and we both knew that I didn't want everyone finding out. We had an unspoken bond that sat behind serious eyebrows when things got a little bit tetchy.

He did everything in his power to inspire and cheer me, chivvying and cajoling at every opportunity. He introduced me to the main university campus, where people were, all the action occurred, and subsidised beer poured freely. A reliable wingman for a convivial drinking pilot, it seemed a reasonable exchange of favours. Happy not to think, and extremely glad of a friend who knew his way about, I followed him blindly to weekly events, wormed my way into the union bar and leeched his social life until I found friends of my own. Officially, music college folks, such as I, weren't really allowed access to university goings-on, but, as wingman, doors opened wide. In return, I'd distract the ugly ones, that was the deal.

Rag week was a disco of opportunity. Everywhere one turned was another eager segment of society colourfully and noisily exercising their right to be recognised. Enthusiasts fought for the best tree-branches and wall-spots to spout their hearty truths. Photocopied posters covered every wall-space, banners blazed, ballasted balloons blew, stickers stuck, tins and sabres rattled.

Student life opened wide myopic curious eyes to realms of unalike thinking, no subject or opinion seemed too outrageous to be beyond the pooling of perspective, principles proliferated in teeny-weeny minds. Mine was full and clogged instantly. Looped mind-knots of previously unthought thoughts clotted the neural processors, inhibiting the carefree fun expected.

It was widely known, at least to me, that, in public, no one ought talk about; sex, religion or politics. Them's the rules. Well, no such luck. With so many new people to accidentally insult all round and about, it was impossible to know who'd defend any particular stance, or the degree to which they'd stand up and fight their corner. Sentences became minefields while pandering to the shifting linguistic bounds of societal obligation. So, I opened my heart up to social justice, taking great cares to refine my language to stop arbitrarily offending others. Exorcising my right to be recognised as a pig-ignorant yokel, with constant reference and deference to peculiar keyhole visions of acceptability, it seemed best, ordinarily, just to say nothing, never make jokes at anyone's expense, ever, and refrain from affecting funny foreign inflection for fear of offending frail Frenchmen. I, for one, boggled at how a single brain could process all the conflicting data in one lifetime. Alongside my death wish, there didn't seem much point trying to get a grip on what *other* people thought, *their* problems *their* own, but, life persists, so, efforts were made to absorb the etymology of the long list of truly offensive words that the rag-week hand-book said not to use, ever, many of which were entirely new to me.

On campus grounds, gay rights, in particular, were being shouted about loudly. Under such a potent onslaught of bright confident happy people, my own chaste misgivings towards sex-out-of-wedlock crumbled like wet biscuit. Empathy: Lesson one. Other people are people too, *all* other people. Om.

I coveted the free and easy way in which they stuck two fingers up at the scriptures, with such a lack of fear of retribution from petty Gods. Lucky buggerers. My God still had me trapped, in fear of breaking a moral code that He still refused to describe in any great detail. Like them, I wanted to tell the world how much I particularly wanted to express myself through sex, only, there was no 'coming out' as straight, no soapbox from which to shout, no flag or gazebo to stand under, no tee-shirt to promote straightness without a misconstrued homophobic undercurrent. No one would ever propose a straight pride festival; given all of history, and that stuff, it seemed to be rather a trifling quibble.

Welcome strangers, passing by with glossy leaflets, brought awareness to the brutal suppression and vile treatment of women, homosexuals, the religious, and various down-trodden peoples of the world. Important stuff. Terrible stuff. Godawful stuff.

As an especially fresh freshman, to witness such passion on tricky subjects was invaluable for the inner schoolboy to learn and grow, emulating earnest language, copying wilful behaviour, noticing courage of conviction and vital vehemence of spirit. although I struggled blinkeredly to understand what a double-bass playing student living on debt could do about any of it.

It felt vaguely disingenuous wandering from group to group agreeing with everyone about everything, but, in an equal world, if another person felt strongly enough about something to shout about it, then, who was I to deny them their position? I wanted to enjoy all the people I met and take in my surroundings gladly, in case of sudden death, which is what I was half-expecting to happen, any, moment, now.   Now.   Now...

Inner peace. Plenty to ponder. Solace could be found in the somewhat Buddhist mantra that; *most* people are *mostly* correct in the thrust of *most* of what they say, *most* of the time, even hippies. So, while the mind whirred endlessly, not quite able to answer cleverly or run away, I nodded through much testament there could be no possibility of my having a valid opinion upon and signed lots of heartfelt petitions I'm not sure that I really agreed with, some of which *clearly* didn't agree with each other. Empathy: Lesson two. People are complex. Om.

Drifting about, private worries and needs were drowned out, lost in a sea of martyrs clinging to some crusade or another. Somehow, in my humourless distrustful state, it felt like these various activists and compassionate bullies demanded of myself, and everyone, that we should stop treating them equally and, instead, raise up their singular troubles in stature above our own so that they may be heard the loudest, much like guitarists.

Before long, bored with fraudulent *bonhomie* beneath brash bombardment, brazen bouts of belligerence began to manifest. No room left in my bristling brain for any more of life's victims; one was quite enough. If the sole purpose of a new interaction was to be a spreading and storing of another's pain and distress as a personal memory, I really *really* didn't want to know, thanks for the kindly offer though.

Unwelcome strangers passing with leaflets brought brutal self-awareness to how very little I cared. I'll take your flyer, and your pamphlet, and yours, sure, I'll take yours too, and yours, but, actually, why don't you save us all a lot of time and effort, the litter bin is over there.

It was all too easy to feel 'got at' in my municipal of mind. Violations? Colonialism? Colon violation? Why don't you talk to the gays about that? I'd mutter angrily, as I mooched through the banner-strewn university campus, chafing under a double entendre, furrowing a deepening groove to the music college.

2: Music College

Famed for vibey jam-sessions with brilliant northern jazzers in its popular bustling late-night bar, the music college, due to some finance issue, and modern hygiene standards, had newly moved, inconveniently, away from all the decent student action to the other side of town, into an obnoxious new-build brick-box that reeked sickeningly of chemical fumes and unwashed youth.

Some distracted architect must've held a grudge against those who'd be using this building, it had clearly been designed by an idiot, or, more probably, a community of idiots. The practice-rooms, for instance, 'specially designed' by an 'acoustic-engineer' had no sound insulation, yet the walls had been angled so that even soft sounds would cut the ears in peaky throbbing slaps of phasing interference.   Drums were very painful, cymbals caused lasting injury. To top that: all windows, in all rooms, in all weathers, had to remain firmly shut, not even a crack, due to noise pollution and being located next to a busy working theatre. One could open the windows, but only when *not* playing music, *in a music college*. The heady bouquet of damp clammy mammals choked the sinuses once while the bleachy vomity paint smells had stopped stinging the eyes and throat. Smoking outside.

The unsubsidised mezzanine café-bar, which also served as the main meeting area for everyone, didn't allow live music in it, *in a music college.* We couldn't believe it. Instead, the sterile, drafty, and often *wet* space, in which they served alcohol, mainly to teenagers, had steep stairs in the centre that fell away sharply. Taking half-pint bets on bruise, blood or bone casualties made for macabre entertainment on rainy days. Uncomfortable low-slung seating had pensive students hunched over expensive *small* drinks, in chilly contemplation of career-ending injury.

Music lessons supplied much needed distraction from the off-putting environment. We had some great teachers, the very best imparters of knowledge and enthusiasm for harmonic growth that the 'world' had to offer, but the few short hours of classes each week were much earlier and less helpful than expected.

Advanced Theory, Harmony, and Composition lessons were, at least at first, remedial, which was a shame. Some of us were already able to read music, some of us weren't; some of us could play our instruments, some of us couldn't; some knew what the teacher was on about, some didn't; some could decipher chord symbols and charts, knew lots of jazz standards, had a history of group performance and were willing to play at any time with anyone, anywhere, for any reason, and some of us weren't.

All the students were at different stages along the musical path, obviously, many much further along it than myself, some had never stepped foot upon it, so, to make sure everyone could keep up, we began from square one. That's fairness, that is, in a *required-attendance,* trudging through town in biting drizzle before dawn to be told what a 'crotchet' is, kind of a way. An exactly equal education. The tutors had good stuff in their brains, useful stuff, chromatic revelations, but they weren't forthcoming, and so started a bitterly slow year for our group to learn that a twelve-bar blues has twelve bars in it, still, I'd made no other life plans.

To my horror, we were expected to write essays *about* jazz. Writing? Seriously? With these blisters? Life skills? No, thanks. Interest in lessons waned, history didn't matter, that'll come, or not, I simply wanted to play, presently. Playing music brought light, no time to wallow in darkness, reactive only to notes and banter thrown about. Eyes tightly shut, hidden behind a double life, lost in colourful swirls that smeared irrelevant thoughts away. Hours, days and weeks would pass in blissful candy-pop dreams, until instantly the biting chill of stark stinking reality would snap back in. Keep the groove, keep the groove, keep the oh.

Hanging out in the vibeless bar with half a pint and a double-bass, plenty of positive people popped up, prepared to prattle on about specific particulars of jazz harmony, solo flow, instrument technique, choice complex chord changes, scales, modes and favourite forms. Suddenly, reasons to stay alive flocked around. Jazz paradise. Nearly everyone needed a half-reasonable double-bass player. With little effort, I'd become a desirable commodity. It felt great, every twenty minutes filled with something new, responsive, and exciting to deal with. Without really thinking, I'd joined a bunch of bands and found myself merrily running about at the whim of a crazy rehearsal schedule for dynamic strangers. Empathy: Lesson three. Some people are brilliant. sOme.

Diary space suddenly at a premium, no time or *need* to think, just turn up and play, like children. Strange and glorious music filled the clammy practice rooms, bedrooms, lounges, hallways, *anywhere*, except my shit house. Wherever I lugged that double-bass, there would always be a musician or two, prepared to spend an hour or two going through favoured tunes, usually after a glass of water and, maybe, a cigarette outside, any excuse to get wet armpits into a breeze. Physically, fingertips were raw, hands bruised, wrists aching, forearms tender, shoulders sore, back niggled with exertion, belly constantly ravenous, fueled by potted pasta and cheap crisps, fatigue had set in deep, I stank like a baked-bean bolognese, but this was living, really living.

However, no profound answers could be found when playing, nor smoking on doorsteps, nor ranting at baffled jazzers over cups of strong unsugared milkless tea, no amount of discussion of, say, diminished scales, or appropriate use of a flat-thirteenth, in over-priced cafés, would ever help answer the intense nagging questions and emotional predicaments that consumed the mind. Philosophically, no matter how many hours spent distracted by music making; no matter how many miles lumbering along grumbling to myself self-righteously, I was getting nowhere fast.

UNIVERSITY OF LOVE   pt.1

3: Xenophobe

Yorkshire was going to be a fantastic place to die. I bumbled about blithely, grinning manically in a cheery upbeat fashion, eyes on the next social event horizon, living for the moment, thrilled to be wedging distance between past and present, relishing the architecture, the crowds, the bars, sniffing flowers, enjoying insects, counting blessings, saying determinedly how good things were, how gladdening it felt to be here on this rock, in this place, at this time, how lucky we were. Come on world, let's have *fun*. Bootstraps grasped firmly, destination: altitude. Positive attitude. Goodly mood. Grinny grin. Groovy groove.

Bad move. For, for many loud social progressives, whose jet-set horizons commanded deference from us young impressionables, there existed a misplaced rage against contentment itself. Folks tolerating their fates were berated or faced weighty debates. Show up, get shown up, show down, get shot down. And repeat. Simply by assuming the accepting position, while attempting to spread sunniness and love to all, I'd unwittingly become the unthinking uncaring ambassador of the cultural oppressor. Who'd've known? Not *I*. Maybe I really was more abrasive than memory allows, maybe my version of jollity tinged with pathos and mild self-hatred fell outside the bounds of normal humour, whatever, it wasn't long before I'd learned the error of my ways; the spread of false jollity: follity, if you will, is purest folly.

Due to past and pending political problems, proud patriotism was perceived as a practice of the poor and stupid. But, but, but *I'm* poor and stupid. Passed about were allegations of willful ignorance being equivalent to wanton criminal negligence, being counterpart to conspiratorial warmongering, being murder.

It is amazing what caffeine can do to a sadist.

Whenever stuck in conversation with such a person, either: one soon loathed oneself for one's silent ignorant responsibility in a long history of warring families, one hated oneself for being powerless to stop the strong eating the weak, one hated oneself for naïvely bending the truth in an attempt to make things seem more agreeable, or one hated oneself for being in the presence of such a vile creature, who'd insist that one hated oneself, whatever one's ambitions were or one's previous actions proved. I'd never known such self-contempt before and didn't care for it much; I'd been trying to let go of self-contempt, if anything. Empathy: Lesson four. Some people aren't brilliant. sOmany.

As a sound-bite, 'intolerance of the intolerable', provided a communal, national and international gold-standard for every personal freedom. No one need listen to offensive strangers. That's part of the bargain in a free society, people can vote with their feet, as at jazz gigs. Off I'd wander under dark clouds, struggling with a heavy internal umbrella, entirely unable to do anything about anything, least of all these moaning minnies.

Oft I'd wonder that things were, things are, things change mainly for the better, whysoever complain? Infancy and idiocy, war and peace, bloodshed and remorse, cruelty and kindness, common sense and civil sense, common law and civil law, civilisation, refinement, revolution, evolution, progress, due process, capital punishment finally a bygone horror, and now, multiculturalism in action, our very freedoms to be guaranteed, not all of the world had come so very very far.

With a reasonable free education system, free health service, free internet on its way; freedom from guns, freedom from natural disasters, deadly diseases, predators and sudden death, (except; Adders, and several varieties of poisonous mushroom that might do the job,) equal liberties for all to shout about themselves through whistling megaphones coming along nicely, Yorkshire, specifically, was perfect, despite the incessant drizzle.

Northern folk generally made for a pleasant enough populace or so it seemed through soft southern eyes. There existed a national togetherness, or near enough, comedic banter thrown about instead of arrows and bayonets, making for a peaceable peacetime, hard won by a long shared interwoven history of absurd wars, despotic kings and mad governors. Truce, through democratic insistence that none should be forced to put up with barbaric nonsense, a general agreement of what constitutes such nonsense historically, and an acceptance to adhere to the expanding body of scientific data that will continue to search out, in ever finer detail, *that* which nonsense itself actually *is*, helped by universal schooling and forced liberalisation of the general populace, folks like me, at the rate that such an elaborate scheme allows for. Drip, drip. Hooray.

Even if no student really knew the true letter of the law, with the infamous 'golden-rules' binding us together in common peaceful purpose, we could be proud of the ever-changing jigsaw of general sensibilities that loosely defined us culturally, and united and protected us constitutionally. In the name of art, especially, everyone was allowed to do anything they wanted to try to get away with, almost, short of actual criminal damage, realisation of one's imagination limited only by one's charm, the financial force one wielded, or the height of one's tree.

How very lucky we were. What a marvellous time to be alive, if that's your thing. Just look at all the lovely people doing anything they want, enjoying their freedom to the fullest. Bravo. Just look at the sophisticates complaining resentfully about the very state of grace in which they are allowed to complain. Boo. Some people can be most ungrateful. Not me. Not patriotic scum, like me. In some ways, 'xenophobe' being leveled as a hippy insult, as something to be ashamed of, made me feel as though I were the only person around with a brain in my head, and, in some other ways, like the only person without one.

Society looked healthy from where I stood, it just seemed a bit odd why some people, who reaped its every advantage, acted like they wanted to dismantle it all from the bottom up, at the very moment when the full benefit of prolonged learning from well-documented errors seemed to be finally taking effect.

Hippies complained a lot about the free press, they still do, there's a lot to complain about; evil has all too often been given a soapbox, and the merest whiff of atrocity can spin nations into a wild frenzy, it's fair enough to moan, a bit, but even so, the free presses stoke the fires of nonsense-spotting, bellowing the good, stamping out the bad, keeping public debate vigorous. To those bad at maths, and equally unused to newspaper tricks, when statistics transmuted into bold hyper-excitable headlines it might've seemed as if we lived in the worst place in the world, when, really, by allowing scandal to be brought to everyone's shocked attention, by displaying failures of thought for all to see, by forcing hot topics down throats until changes happened, free speaking societies weren't failing to deal with their thorny issues, quite the opposite. But it took time. Change always took time. More time than I had to give, now mere months and counting.

I'd never be the great man once willed into being, I'd never take on the rotten institutions, theocracies and all corrupt office. *I* couldn't get it together enough to understand anything fully, because around every corner there'd always be a pedantic arsehole attempting to derail trains of thought by throwing chains of irrelevant meaning across the tracks of reasonable conversational scope. The bastards. Words of power and import would have to be left to the academics, politicians, journalists, authors, songwriters and poets, maybe poets, I'd nothing to add to the great lexicon. I'd found my level, distilling the overwhelming into handy manageable sound-bites of simple instruction. If it's good enough for the free press, desk-diaries, all Buddhist philosophy, and most other religious texts, then it's plenty good enough for me.

4: The Scottish Problem

My girlfriend had moved to Scotland to study. I still loved her *very* much, to the point of obsessive hysterical possession. She was all I had. All I wanted. All my heart desired. All I allowed myself to think or talk about. Critically, we were still waiting.

Majestic family futures we'd defined in detail at the start of our relationship left us with dozens of promises to keep or break. Keenly had I tied myself to the restrictions of our plans, but then those best-laid plans had been, quite literally, buggered.

I often phoned her student halls. Too often. Bills became a worry.   Weekly budgets wasted waiting querulously, quietly, impatiently, for a randomised Scottish student to announce that she wasn't, in actual fact, around. No need to rub it in, I thought. I'd had invisible friends before, most unsatisfactory.

When she *did* answer, I found myself confounded, flustered and frustrated at her lack of enthusiasm. Admittedly, yearning to be in her thoughts as often as she filled mine was acutely slim hope indeed, but I craved equivalence. It hurt that she wasn't equally crippled by our distant love, so I'd fish for assurances, pushing her to be similarly neurotic. Go on, say it, *I'll* say it, I lo... Words didn't come easily.   I rarely knew the real meaning of most sounds flying out of the mouth or into the ears. Half of all inference was feeling. More than half. Probably more than that. Raw uproar and passion, where faith, hope and love abide, and psychosis also. Several times we ended our chats with: well, we'll just have to wait and see what happens then, won't we? ClkuuuuuuuuuuuuuuuuuuuuuuuuuuuuuuuuuuuIloveyouuuuuuu.   Sniff. Which, in some ways, is simply horrendous, in other ways, a test, a challenge to be noble, or, possibly, a free-ticket kindly given, certainly a most stultifying moral dilemma for a horny teenager.

Sadness filled the flesh; so much sadness I revelled in it and wrapped myself in its cold embrace, hoping it'd take me one step closer to the end. Nnnnngh, okay, fine, next time, when *next* on the phone, *then* death by broken heart on the hallway stairs.

Being left to fend for oneself in a new town persists as a very romantic notion and all; start a new life, settle down, create a family, build a home, a shed, something for a determined youngster to get eager teeth into, however, while enduring an empty bed under the onslaught of five noisy nymphomaniacs and thin walls, whilst she remained so very very far distant, for *some* reason the promised thrill of adventure escaped me.

She'd no plans to visit for she was busy, and nor would her student halls allow for me to stay, and she'd said not to go, also, which smarted a bit. Forcing myself upon her after a spoken 'no' was not on. I knew that much. I'd been told. But, in my head, looking back bleakly, or forward forlornly, darkness covered the skyline. I mused upon her, upon us, upon choices generally, our bonded psychic union as warm sunshine upon closed eyelids.

Starry-eyed isolation had the brain in overdrive, grandiose plans were crafted to turn up and propose with a platinum ring, roses, champagne, hotel-suite and romance. Say 'no' to *that*. Except I'd no ring or roses, no champagne, no way to transform plans into reality. Trains and hotels *way* too costly, no time to return in a day by bus, banned from driving, the long cold walk to Scotland the only option to allow the potential sowing of wild Oates. Sleeping rough on a Scottish street in winter appealed in *one* way, the unrequited romance of a sad, silent, frozen death.

Restless on grubby bed-sheets, failing to sleep, smoking cigarettes irritably, I'd cry a lot, like a man, a normal man, a teenage man, arguing all night with her, and God, in a pleading, huffy, puffy-headed whimper, snivelling into the pillow, grizzling until Tupperware skies meant leaving the house with weighty double face and fool's golden smile to continue the chirpy charade.

Still no ambition, no future plans as such, a jazzer meanwhile, as rubbish an example of humanity as existed anywhere, conviction grew that she needed her freedom from me, easily as much as I did. I still missed her, but now *required* reassurance, or closure. Wise girl housemates advised face-to-face only for closure. I agreed reticently, phone calls had become painful, my language skills insufficient for such a harrowing ordeal.

She decided to stay in Scotland for Christmas, so that answered that. Perceptions askew, options few, doubts nagged away, assurance wasn't forthcoming. Follity and love. Bumble along humming. There didn't seem much point to 'ought else; why bother? I'd definitely be dead by summer. Definitely definite.

Time drudged on, winter passed, cherry blossoms bloomed, hollow promises resonated. Head full of nonsense, ears full of noise, sap rising fast, the eyes opened wide to the abundance of girls, hundreds, thousands, but none special enough to replace *her* in my mind, after all, we were, at the end of the day, waiting, together, to be, potentially, married. It's a certain life-choice. Certain. If one stays pure of spirit, at least one will have always had that to be glad about. Thankfully, at some point soon, while still chaste, still eligible for heaven, the ribcage would explode and bloody innards burst asunder, poisoned by the venom of embittered loneliness, any, moment, now. Now. Now...

Now. Oh *come on!* An army of kittens clawed the gullet at every fleeting thought of her absence, every unobserved effort ground away at the soul, no glory to be found, no fluidity of spirit, nothing. Head treacle oozed glacially, living each hour paralysed, looping sadly in the emotional climax of a cheesy love song.

The situation proved too intense for my very little brain. Howling with loneliness in that cold, damp, putrified room, I cursed geography, the cost of phones, cost of travel, cost of platinum rings, pined for a close companion as a puppy might and, without really meaning to, began to mourn our relationship.

UNIVERSITY OF LOVE   pt.1

5: Splurge

Determined to stop the rot, hardy bootstraps holding firm, plans went into overdrive to find an excess of pleasure that'd bring this unceasing barrage of gloomy gobbledygook to an end tolerably. Cider and cigarettes, the papers advertised credible things about liver and lung disease that I wanted to put to the test. I started saving the golden packets and stacked them up the wall with the intention of making a suit. The golden suit never happened, sad to say, I couldn't afford to smoke enough, the stack of empty boxes stood only as a reminder of the money spent, how many metres of fivers burned away, however, I *did* make a golden top hat, with the plan of wearing it to house parties.

Parties, where real education happens, the best chance to shine, to display the true nature of the soul to pretty acquaintances, meet fellow students, prod and poke each other, debate the ins and outs of topics beyond comfortable frames of reference, and get so completely smashed that none could stand. Hooray.

Armchair governors in waiting, waxy guests waned lyrical, playing the various vicarious victims to imagine what suffering might feel like, pompously advocating how life *should* be lived, how difficulties *should* be overcome, attempting to out-liberalise each other with ever-loftier opinions, pinning a close variance of a favourite parent's colours to some mast or other, questioning possible routes through very recently acquired knowledge.

In that harrying environment, loosened on economy alcohol, caught in a ceaseless torrent of righteous guff I cared not for, woeful tales of personal defilement would suddenly splurge forth in a morbid frenzy wholly unbecoming of a normal human being. Sadly, it appeared that my drunken self was intolerant of anyone who'd decided that they wanted to play the victim unnecessarily.

When intoxicated, the slightest thing could spark an episode as I'd filter everything through a victim's sieve in order to hammer any disagreeable lumps into a fine dust. Soberly accustomed to holding 'it' back, to keep 'it' hidden from view, I'd find myself waiting expectantly to use 'it' as a conversational weapon, a defensive trip-switch, a trump card of victimhood with which to beat away noisy people who pushed the buttons a bit too much. I became hardened to the sudden look of panic that would land as they'd scrabble desperately for some soft platitude or other.

Usually, when it became known that I'd been dishonoured recently, in an unspeakable sense, most people would express pity, anger, and disbelief on my behalf. Though I didn't want pity and had plenty enough anger for us all. A big strapping lad like you? Yep, I was roofied. Oh? Yeah. Oh. Yeah. Oh! Yeah.

Parties, generally, aren't the best place for counselling, but people like to have a wild stab at it, to show caring. Bless 'em. Many males had stories to tell, but most didn't, lip-biting, fighting an inner-seal of confessional. Many females said that I was lucky not to have been impregnated, which remains a valid point, although, one could argue, not a very helpful point, at all, in fact, quite the opposite. When lump hammering, I could only hear of my 'good luck' from the mouth of an actual victim, not as petty point-scoring against *all* men, for *I'm* a man, and, yet, a victim. Empathy: Lesson five. Sympathy is not empathy. metoOmetoo.

After I'd been calmed and mollycoddled for a while, away from the group, it would often be difficult to return to the crowds, so, thanks, bye; quiet escape hiding the leaky eyes, pretending that another invite needed attending to, as the sea of eyebrows would rise in a tide to see the nutter safely out of the room.

Back to the shell. Back to the denial denying den. Back to the hell of myriad menial problems sobbing through the system, holding the head, moulding the bed, wishing for swift death, squeezing bodily liquids into thin loo-roll and pungent bedding.

As coping strategies went, while so determined to drink to demise, *attempting* to ignore 'it', but, in so doing, *failing* to ignore 'it', was no good for my health or for people nearby. My drunken self, a pitiable creature, could not be trusted to keep it shut. Bottling up thoughts through mindless distraction, and 'letting shit go', over time, had only served to fabricate a high-velocity cork of boozy botch and bungle. This wasn't peace. This wasn't harmony. This wasn't the joyful bettering of self that'd been promised by the liberated carefree hippies I'd been trying to emulate.

A positive change of tact was needed to get 'it' out of the way, so that 'it' needn't come out later. I restrategised, telling people 'it' sober, out of context, at the first opportunity. Unsuspecting friends would introduce me to their friends, who would then either leave immediately with wrinkled temples, or would stand shaking their necks, tutting, which became extremely awkward for everyone in the room, so that strategy bore no fruit either.

Disharmony seemed to be spreading all around me, from me, concentrically, and not *just* from experimental daily jazzing. Booze? Blame the booze. Silence swept through my heart again. Sobriety didn't cut it either, I really needed decent curative meds, a drug to help keep the wild creature inside hushed until death.

They call it dope for a good reason. Grass, weed, bud, hash, whatever we could get, whatever was cheap, worked a treat. From a rich trombonist friend I borrowed: Vlad the Inhaler, a five-foot bong needing two people to work it, then set about keeping medicated away from the snooty gaze of party people. The beast restrained, the priest retrained, peace, love, laughter and patience returned. The daily grind had a smoother sanding-wheel installed, dreams became less stressful, acceptance of all things shitty became darkly humorous once more, people became less stressful too, distance passed under the feet quicker, life eased, all in all, I'd found my drug of choice. Thank you God for marijuana, please legalise it, and make it cheaper, Amen.

UNIVERSITY OF LOVE   pt.1

6: Buddha and the Tortoise

Free living blew itself out almost immediately. The few quid available without effort had long ago been pissed up the wall or burned to ash, zero had become a long forgotten daydream; the bottommost reaches of sanctioned borrowing, a reinforced glass carpet, my form sprawled spread-eagle across it. All a loan did was pay off other debts, bought a lump, filled the fridge, and allowed for a few heroic nights of fiscally unfeasible wingmanship. Bills loomed ominously. Frugality reigned.

Big ideas of perishing bearably evaporated, sober penury coalesced. Dying young, in poverty, widely respected, that *was* still the only plan, but it wasn't as easy as it sounded, with cash so scarce, paid work so rare, and music *literally* time and effort. It'd have to be starvation or exhaustion, not drug-abuse, shame. Immortality on a compact disc would have to suffice for impact, all I now had to do was record the best jazz album ever, the more obscure the better, *then* die, *then* they'd be proud, or impressed, or sorry, or something. Admittedly, it wasn't a perfect theory.

Sculpting low frequency noise had the benefit of being a free pastime, moving about, however, became a problem, Yorkshire being only hillocks, hummocks and gradients. Shifting a double-bass and, often, large amplifier, around the city by foot was an exhausting, slow and smelly business.   Buses were a luxury that 'wasn't beer', were generally insufficient for luggage needs, and mostly full to the brim on rainy days. Taxis were right out.

In truth, the college *did* have some half-reasonable double-basses available, but college policy stated that a first year student wouldn't get a good one, and they didn't all have pick-ups, so *most* weren't band functional. Nor could a college-bass or amp be taken off of college-grounds. Bass-guitar? Um, no, thanks.

Inspired by skater housemates, when the last loan instalment arrived, I invested in skateboard wheels, trucks, and bearings, attached them to the bottom of my combo amp with big screws, tied a headscarf around the handle and, with the bulky double-bass slung over the shoulder, wheeled it along like a play-buggy. It required torque to get moving, upward slopes troublesome, but with a bit of grit the city was mine to gig without the necessity of staggering back'n'forth carrying equipment being the only thing done all day. Sat atop the rolling amp, the double-bass held like a jousting lance, I'd ride any gentle slope. Gleeful. Genuine pleasure on tarmac. Paving and cobbles, much less so.

I'd found an identity: that bare-legged bloke with the double-bass, pit rings, and amp on wheels. Sure, I'd tried long trousers, but due to heat of effort burning muscles, legs would stream and steam on even the coldest, driest of days. Steaming legs cool more efficiently exposed. Plus, bare skin wipes clean after rain, whereas trousered skin remains soaked through. Shorts. Yeah.

Carrying burdens around everywhere took its toll. Hungry, tired, skew-whiff, smelly, shattered and semi-conscious all day, every day, after not very long at all the body started to break. If I'd known fatigue and blisters were prerequisites for a double-bass player I'd've learned the flute, but no one tells you that on the application forms. Sores, sciatic twinges, hobbling hips, weak knees, plantar fasciitis, verrucas, styes, warts and gum-boils, the physique manifested the psyche, step by step by heavy step.

I'd disconnect from aches, float above the pain, enjoy the rain, ignore the physical strain, swing from a skyhook, imagining hosts of Holy angels raising me up. Detached from circumstance, from abrasions and bunions, from memories past, a new man reassembled every moment, I nodded and winked to anyone new, waved salutation to everyone I knew, mostly with a sweet smile and the lightest of dispositions, while trudging past sweaty, pained and gasping. Ahaha, yes, what a sight, I'm sure. Om.

One day, on my way through town with more equipment than a human should carry, I met a chap sat cross-legged on a traffic island crossing, he seemed nice, friendly, and so I plonked my stuff down next to him, above and around him. After ten long minutes of his sob story, I gave him a fiver, not much in the grand scheme of things, but several day's budget, and all I had.

I strode on, pretty chuffed with this new charity therapy, a wash of pure joy poured through me as I bounced down the hill. This feeling must be the Holy Spirit that I'd failed to find in church, I thought to myself, smugly. Letting go of the right things. Yay.

Next day, on the regular trudge into town with the double burden shouldered, I saw him exiting a large mansion house. He was wearing the grin of the sexually satisfied, had a four-pack of good beer tucked under each arm and was rolling a cigarette from a full ounce-pouch of tobacco. It seemed he'd had some luck. I hugged myself just a little bit, truly glad for him, pleased that happiness flourishes in the world if only one puts it out there, out there. Buddha would be happy, *pleased* even, Jesus too. Yay.

With a spring in my step, I waved, nodded and winked as we walked concurrently up to his gate. The very moment I opened my mouth to speak he asked if I had any cash, which I didn't, because I'd given it to him. He didn't recognise me. The double-bastard on my back didn't spark his memory. The hair, bleached and dyed funny colours by bored housemates, didn't trigger a single synaptic twitch. My telling him directly that we'd met yesterday brought only shakes of his head and a disdainful sneer.

As I shuffled off, he insulted selfish students discourteously and loudly at my back. I barely felt the leather strap biting into the flesh. Innate moralism pushed once more to its bitter edge, Buddha could fuck right off; shells, staffs and soul-mates all.

I missed a valuable lesson that day. Playing the double-bastinado for a living is more strenuous and less profitable than begging.

UNIVERSITY OF LOVE   pt.1

7: Help Desk

Each new morning, I would awaken anxious and miserable, evermore surprised by my continued pouting existence. If I had to consider myself one of the 'lucky few', as I'd been told I must, then the shit-bomb of corporeal reality for the 'unlucky many' *proved* the existence of a specifically cruel and malicious deity.

One of the fortunates, here on a shared Earth, an equally vital fraction of humanity, or not, ready to make an equal share of impact upon this planet, or not, tick tock. Searching for calm ferociously, I had a really long hard look at myself, reaffirming physical persistence in the grotty bathroom mirror, a reflection of a shadow of a piquant man, under bad lighting, and yet, the occasional flash, a shiny twinkle of *something* behind the eyes. Hope? Wit? Cruelty? Malevolence? Stupidity? Difficult to tell.

Disquieting humours lay upon me, for the first time I *knew* that I knew nothing useful. Questioning all things only works if one asks the right questions. Finally, I admitted to needing help. In order to pass time constructively, I tracked down a student-run help-desk for victims of rape, open for a few hours, once a week. I skipped a lesson and made the journey to see if they had anyone to talk to about quelling the appalling turmoil within, or, indeed, if I could help out at all making teas and coffees, and stuff. Having had some experience in these matters, I thought it would be nice to turn my hand to volunteering, to hang out, to join the crowd to shout about my own major topic of concern.

Upon arrival, the militant anti-man immediately suggested that I was there to 'turn myself in'. They were probably meaning to be funny. I didn't get it. In fact, I exploded in a violent rage, kicking up a rumpus like they'd never seen. I couldn't stop it. Hooooow? Fuuuuucking! Daaaaare! Yooooou?

The top blew off of my cranial thermometer. Irate, spitting with petulant incredulity through a watery blur, I demanded an apology, a written apology, not just from my accuser but from the head of the student body, the Dean, the Governors, the Chair of the University, the damned Secretary for Education. I wanted grovelling, I wanted it *here*, there, and I wanted it *now*, then, instantly. At which, they stated that they were sorry for the fact that I'd not had it explained to me how hard it was for women to have their safe spaces in the world, and, at length, that *that* office wasn't really the best environment for men, sorry, but you should leave, *now*, some of the ladies might feel uncomfortable.

My testosteronometer popped its gauge. Pupescent with rage, I stood quaking in my boots, grasping a pair of newly broken bootstraps, one in each tightly clenched fist. Daggers were glared and glared back, and glared again for far longer than intended, as a thousand nasty rasping thoughts failed to find purchase. Consciousness crumpled into a paper ball with all the precise words of rebuttal penned upon its hidden folds. Nnnnnnngh!

Calm. Calm! Public displays of angst and idiocy weren't in the master plan. Primary objective: to find a tolerable calm. Are you gonna leave, or shall I call security? Breathe. Breathe! Stammering something about 'it' happening to boys too, I stood clutching at my spiralling head, effing and blindly pushing out a tear or two, the sight of which brought a flicker of fretfulness, though far too late for me, flush with effrontery, I flounced off in a furious huff and a half, foaming with effervescent fury, following a famous formulaic format of shameful fuckwittery.

Hope remained that they *might* later feel guilty for misreading the situation so obviously and obliviously, and, therefore, *maybe,* might possibly treat the next male passerby with a little more respect, or less abuse, or not be so swift to judge, or something, but it seemed unlikely. *They* were why people *should* complain. If *they* represented *my* issues, then the system needed a reboot.

I hit a wall. There seemed little point going back or taking complaints further. They, for all their faults, were trying to help. Just because they couldn't help, and rubbed me up the wrong way, and then offended the very root of what I consider to be me, they hadn't intentionally meant any harm, they were just stupid, more stupid even than me, and yet, in charge of a help desk.

Maybe, just maybe, and no more, maybe I *couldn't* die just yet, *maybe* I'd like to leave the world marginally better than it was when I found it, *maybe* there could still be enough time to make a tiddly-tiny punctum on the infinite plane of all existence.

Maybe, just maybe, if this unearthed charge of emotional static could be redirected to battle a deserved enemy, *then* life *might* be fruitful, *maybe*, even worthwhile, *maybe*. Maybe.

Maybe taking up boxing would help alleviate some tension.

Maybe smashing fists against walls is a better, cheaper, more immediate alternative to unaffordable gyms.

Maybe broken knuckles wouldn't help anything.

Maybe that should have been thought about earlier.

Maybe it had been.

Maybe a major blood vessel will burst if ire fire is allowed to flow unchecked for another single horrid minute, nnnnngh, maybe *this* minute, nnnnngh, maybe *this* minute, nnnnngh.

Maybe by tomorrow it'll all be over and this will be the last thought I'll ever have, goodnight cruel world, oh, it's dawn.

A hapless mess of an exhausted man, I soon became my own super-anti-hero, with the classic useless alter-ego, triggered into action by raging injustice, the backstory had written itself.

If you have a problem, if no one else can help, and if you can find him, maybe you can hire: Rapeboy, the victim's victim. Yay. Out for violent painful revenge should it ever happen to pass by. Give him a difficulty, and he'll stare out of the window, or at it, and pointedly try to think of something else, maybe compose a morbid poem, if he can hold the pencil in his mangled paw.

8: Floristry

To repair my carbuncular soul, I required someone to hold, kiss, and share sunsets, now, tonight. Romance would save me. Reciprocated love. Sympathetic love. Passionate love. But, critically, most important of all, local love.   If another perfect person came along to have luvvyduvvy conversations with, *then* there'd be a singular reason to blunder through each unrelenting, unremitting, remorseless, incessant bloody day.

Temptations of the flesh called loudly from women liberally distributed, and even though I kept my eyes to myself, or to other eyes, with hormones raging, synapses blazing, and sheer weight of numbers, I fell in lust hourly, finding no inner or outer peace because of it. Having told friends that I was taken, under assumption of harsh judgement, I started to regret that choice while lolloping about town with my tongue hanging out.

Thoughts of my officially unofficial girlfriend stayed my hand. I think, therefore: *blam!* Knots of self-loathing in the gut, clots of guilt in the mind. I didn't want to let 'us' down, yet I didn't want to die before popping that cherry. Dreams were as being stretched, squeezed and disemboweled by mad feral Banshees. Surely, a love shared is a love doubled, not a cold rejection of it, I'd try to convince myself, unsurely, but whether or not celibacy out-of-wedlock *would* or *wouldn't* guarantee entry into heaven, it is a matter of integrity. Virginity is a deeply scored barrier that one cannot cross twice, once across, there's no turning back, I wasn't truly convinced that I wanted to so casually toe that line.

Robbed of the mountings broody adolescence anticipated, occupied lamentably, lost amidst unceasing invasive onslaught. As at Dunkirk, ships had sailed, seamen backed up the lines, from Mardick, to Coxyde, rescue craft required directly.

Amongst the general free-love meat market, which all of my housemates were enthusiastically making much loud energetic use of, I couldn't deny that I'd fallen for a fair few fair maidens, handpicked by eyeball for shared passions and likely reciprocal desires. Over time, improbably, several even warmed to me.

In university environs, with the music turned up fractionally too loud and everyone shouting at each other, hours wiled away intermingling with all, accepting of my purpose as wingman, distracting the insufferable, holding court to share a moan with the difficult. I was content, to a point; that adverse unhappiness that develops when drained of duty and obligation to platonic relationships with the spiritually misshapen. Enough is enough, ask anyone. Empathy: L6. Some people just won't fuck off. Omg.

Slyly, lying to myself, 'practicing', I'd wrangle my way next to favourite pretty people and, against God's will, boldly attempt to flirt, puritan style. Twitching neurones interacting with the most aesthetically pleasing in the room; fair forgivable flirtation, yeroner. I didn't know if they wanted me hounding them or not, I didn't much care, I was young, ebullient and maybe a bit tipsy, besides, I, myself, wished many people would stop bothering *me*. There's no variance of gender. No is no, thanks. Don't ask again. In a crowd of such lecherous activity, polite suggestion to meet up to get food together won over a few of the softer hearts.

Friendships would be built up slowly, then, at some point, loud tummy gurgles earned an invite to dinner, nudge nudge wink, bring pyjamas. The suggestions were apparently genuine. Vampires, thresholds, protocol. I made no similar offers. Mine? No. No way. No how. Not a chance. Not ever. Never. Nope.

I'd scrub myself salubrious, turn up with flowers and booze, eat, drink, stay up late nattering happily, playing games, I'd try my best to act distracting, charming, amusing, or whatever, until summoned to bed to 'sleep' for the night, as the boy chosen, from all other potential boys, to stay. Chip, chip. Hooray.

Oh no. At the first offers I freaked out. Thanks for the food. Bye. Slam. Home, shell, bed. But, after one has kicked one's own butt in a lonely bed only a very few times, one learns courage. Learning how to say 'yes' began a new journey along a path of possibility, so bravely *would* stay over, but, typically, nary touch in anxious adjacency, as if an icy wind had chilled the soul.

After such nights, it seemed right to hug and nuzzle for a bit. We'd kiss softly, gently, shyly, slowly improving my technique, there'd always be a sexually quizzical moment of some sort to ruin.   Then the moment would pass and we'd both know it. Okay, sleep well. Yeah, you too, *um*. What? Er, oh, nothing.

I'd made sure they were keen and single, made it painfully clear that I was keen and unburdened for what we had in mind, we'd put in all the hard work together, done the flirtation thing, played all the tricky games of modern humanity well enough to have found ourselves smiling across at each other in bed, yet, speaking for myself, I couldn't nudge any one of them 'over the line', nor, seemingly, would I be nudged, neither.

In such a world heaped with sexual expectations, and none, there can exist no precise way to evaluate what a woman expects from a man, or, more specifically, at that moment, from me. Probably nothing, as the feminists would quite rightly have it. No one wants the trouble of a pesky male bothering them when trying to sleep, I certainly didn't, and yet, as a pesky male, all that enwrapped every thought was how best to achieve orgasm.

A rutting man-boy in peak sexual prime, an alluring favoured physical form half-naked within arm's reach, filling the nostrils, there existed no other bio-chemical teenage focus. It felt to me, somewhere in the back and front of my mind, that our being there together had forced fate's hand, all I needed to do would be to let loose the beast and allow nature to speak its piece. But no. Courage lacking, I couldn't have been any more respectful if I'd manifested as a potted funeral shrub in a cassock.

Have they suddenly switched path? Have I? How do I find out? Is it because I've been acting weirdly? Am I acting weirdly? They *do* know I'm keen, right? Am I too keen? Have I let slip that I'm a victim? Did they find out from someone else? If so, who? Could they tell anyway? Is their acceptance of me based on sympathy? Empathy? Are they on a path to try to understand or repair me? What are they thinking? What are they thinking? What are they *thinking*? *Maybe* they're waiting for me to leave. Why can we not act upon something so likely to be beautiful? Could it be my ugly hands? Up close they were not a pretty sight.

My suppurated leprous hands weren't wandering anywhere. Unfortunately, pus-flushed flesh, blistered, popped and peeled fingertips were the bane of my love-life, or *a* bane. The double-bassist's curse. Unsmoothable skin edges would snag and catch sharply on nylon or polyester, or spandex, or silk, or satin, or lace, or anything that might ever be worn to please. Flesh on flesh fared no better, scritchscratching delicate areas as chemical stings of biological bustle burned the exposed hypodermis.

Not being a robot, and never wanting to turn away, I'd caress exposed flesh sensitively, with the back of a fist, in hope of recognition and reciprocation; it seemed rude not to after our fun-filled evenings. But. For how many seconds can one person touch another, without clear response, before 'affectionate' becomes 'creepy'? Not long in my mind. Maybe not at all.

Spooning became a cautiously chaste affair; under the false premise of thermo-cooling, I'd move my hips away from any close interaction to hide raging erections. Surely I'd get a slap and a lawsuit if I pushed contact in the middle of a cuddle without first getting married, or, at the very least, engaged.

Over and over, cursing shyness, querying every infinitesimal movement, spasms of intrusive thoughts were hidden by moving a pensive arm slowly, an inch at a time, to where it might rest, somewhere just beyond the bounds of open suggestiveness.

Muted alarm became sirens. Tender brain-cells flipped out. Empathy capacitors inverted. Bubbles of mind goo imploded. No precedent or justification could be found from first principles to action, for any action, whether that was as innocent as to cup a breast, or to merely suggest a late night activity to do together.

The main issue was that I didn't want to be seen to be manipulating the situation, yet obviously wanted to influence the outcome. I needed permission to act, but how to go about asking for it politely completely flummoxed me. I wasn't going to ask for anything directly with mouth words, in case an accusation of unseemly manoeuvres could be leveled at me, for, to be seen to be wanting sex, by asking for it directly, would prove guilt of forethought, which was illegal for men, or heading that way, or something. Lacking for trust, the very idea of false accusations of unwanted manipulation filled the gills with terror. Thoughts of flirtations and intimacies misquoted as evidence of malintent by lawyers in a courtroom skewered icicles through the heart.

Yet here we were together in *their* bed. Could it be that it was *I*, *myself*, a dumb male, no less, being so wantonly manipulated? I'd heard that women could be clever like that, I was rather hoping, ears strained, tumid with anticipation. Maybe they'll offer themselves in a minute. Maybe I will. The mind whirred.

In those lonely moments spent together with familiar girls, I remember feeling envy for the club owner who'd had his fun, because at least he'd had the emotional wherewithal to act on his impulses. For good or ill, at least he'd actually done something in his sordid shitty life, I couldn't even frott properly with people who wanted me lying there next to them, who'd gone out of their way to make it happen. It seemed wrong that *he* should get to have the fun bit while catatonic nightmares of emotional castration filled *me* up. The animosity would build. Grr, I should never be thinking about him, the cunt, never, ever, never ever, never ever *ever*, *especially* not here in a girl's bed.

I'd lay there at a thousand miles an hour, like a head with the chicken cut off. Immobilised by philosophical plate spinning. Correct motivation to act 'properly' as a man in a feminised world, with dignity, integrity, respect, love, tenderness, and a healthy orgasm rate, still baffled and eluded me. Without diversion of some sort I'd only simmer, boil over, flinch and kick out, so, while distracting the brain from self-pity, I'd most often take this opportunity to dismantle the conception of whether 'inaction' could be a 'moral act' if initial intent had been to act immorally. Solace of some sort, I suspect. Judge, jury and executioner; self-convicted, heavily guarded, constrained, restrained and restricted by penal codes of cruel devising, loosely assembled from Biblical Scripture, the Laws of the Land, empirical data, Darwin, my mother, and a death wish; mashing them together confusedly, attempting the interminably toilsome task of unpicking a working ethics from the mind-knot of a horny teenage brain in a single night, without reference books, while over-stimulated bodily, playing footsie, fighting back hormonal reality with the all too real threat of rape charges rarely out of the thoughts. This way and that. It probably wasn't the best time to start tackling such deep issues, but hey ho, gotta start somewhere.

The thought that my own invading manipulators would live forever in a similar jail of mind held some small comfort for me. I imagined maliciously that they'd wake up every single day crippled by the awareness that a well-placed phone call could wreck their names and lives in a finger-snap, that any day the full power of the judiciary could take away everything they love, dragged backwards through the courts for years. This horrid fear of sexual harassment charges hanging over them was their punishment from me. I revelled spitefully in how it felt so very *very* rotten. Good. And yet, self-punishment would only work if they held the same ethical views on what constituted acceptable behaviour as I did, which they most definitely did not. Bad.

With bottom lip quivering, I'd relive every second of my reaching manhood. All at once. Blam. And then again. I couldn't imagine a world where *all* men were required to be raped, to make them act flaccidly to women through a din of hateful memory and a hyper-empathic fear of future reprisal. It didn't seem a foolproof logic to be fed to schoolboys. It didn't seem like it could be rolled out nationally without somebody noticing and complaining. It still worked, sure, but entirely devoid of virtue.

The words didn't come, trailing logical threads were unclear, but somehow, deep down, I felt I'd justified it all by arriving back at the 'right' place anyway. Despite very best efforts, I'd reached puritanism via the back routes, emasculated by a brain full of contradictory rules and conflicted misunderstandings.

After much infernal debate, a draft conclusion found *all* glib sound-bitten advice to be insufficient to live by. Including that. Each individual word choice, stressful speculatively interpreted hyperbolic steps into a future memory-muddle of entanglement, parp, every original realisation accompanied by a discordant chorus of blaring tubas that'd wipe the mind clean of all mental constructs, to start building again from flashes, faces, phantasms, befuddled foresights, first and furthermost fundamental truths.

Truth? *Truth?* Bah. Mathematical certainty in set bounds, sure, absolutely, but a truth of words is almost entirely nonsense. Just because someone said something is so, doesn't make it true. Just because anyone says anything is so, doesn't make it true. Just because God wishes it, simply wasn't good enough reasoning any more, scripture didn't allow for the tweak of common sense. Just because the government, or a friendly hippy says so, wasn't entirely sound thinking either, on a whole variety of scale sets. Just because *I* say so, probably not. But why not? Reasons for laws held inside other heads were, what? Better than mine? Golden? Do as you'd be done by. Easy. I want sex, like every solitary ancestor ever did, even the particularly religious ones.

The minutes ticked by, unable to contextualise any of it. Hour. And a half. Two hours. And a half. Three. A dour huff would flare behind a clenched smile. Tensions would rise. Sleep? Not a chance. Where's my equilibrium? Where's my equilibration? Hmmm? Calm. Cool. Cork. Quiet. Empathy. bOmb. Hmmm.

Turn away. Turn away. Okay, there we go, pressure off. Any moment now they'll spoon-cuddle *me*, any, moment, now. Now. Wow. A hand on the chest, briefly, pectoral muscles tensed hard. Hugging. Horizontal hugging. Why couldn't I yet instigate that easy thing? Why are tits so untouchable? Eh? Tit nipples. That's why. Tit nipples, bra-straps and fear. Fortissimo tubas to wipe thoughts away. First flash, face of effing arrrrrgh!

Impassive behaviour patterns, caused by bubbling internal conflict and over-thinking were a great contraceptive, probably for the best, criminal law blah blah blah, but, as a rutting male in the throws of heat, not really for the best at all. The end doesn't justify the means, when the means is tortuous turmoil, aching heart, insatiability, body and mind straining frustratedly at the failure to behave naturally, as a primal primate might.

While my housemates, and almost everyone else, were at it like lemurs; lawlessly, lecherously, lewdly, lengthily, loudly, limberly, luridly, lucidly, lovingly, luckily, liberally, liberatedly, and leaden-footedly, I required polite, slow, detailed explanation as to what I'd been doing wrong, some handy hints and tips to guide and instruct which idiosyncrasy to address in order to better my chances for next time. Yet, all pre-chewed sound-bites were insufficient, I'd progressed *that* far, seemingly backwards.

On the rare beautiful occasions my gnarly, rough, barnacled hand would be gripped and held warmly, delicate hearts would leap, at least a dozen of them in my chest alone, all clenched tensions would sag and slump immediately, allowing a relieved anxious little boy to drift off into the sweetest of dreams, connected in mind, soul, and spirit, a happy farty monkey.

The following day, the usual suggestion would be that I was gay, which stung a bit, but there you go. Too gay? Too feminine? Me? Really? *Me?* Novel ideas to absorb along with the deluge.

In the cold light of morning, it so transpired that half of them would've, if only I'd've asked, they told me so, in my guise as a probable gay, and I lost yet more sleep to kicking. In a race of one man, I'd managed to come in second, the only consolation found was in blaming *them* for *my* 'failures'; *they* didn't want *me*, *they* didn't push for it, *they* weren't in the mood, and *they* weren't responsive. Primary survival strategy as a rutting male: to remove self from failure. Likewise, half of them wouldn't've, which persists as a great reprieve all round, as far as keeping sex-offences off a criminal record for coin-flipping is concerned. Naturally, *I* didn't want *them*, *I* didn't push for it, *I* wasn't in the mood, and *I* wasn't responsive. Primary survival strategy.

I felt that I could've been trusted to leave these friends sexily unviolated without being trussed to solemn inertia by God, or His Laws, or any other imposed rules crowding in on personal and private interrelations, I'd've responded to 'no', the word is easy enough to understand, I'd become hyper-sensitive to it, but I hadn't thus far had a proper 'no' to respond to, I'd not yet created a situation where anyone had found the need to say it.

They probably weren't attracted to me at close-quarters, with smoky lager breath, wonky teeth, teenage skin, spots, shocking anti-humour, angsti-intellectualism, and natural odour exuding from the pores. That'll be it, *that's* much more likely, and totally fair enough, I couldn't possibly be *too* gay, could I? Not me, surely. Whatever, it needed correcting, so that I might lose my virginity before I died, by year's end, as promised.

Once or twice, invited back with expectation renewed, impetus regained, knowingly on a certain promise. Snap. Double the pressure, twice the failure. No breast cupped, no fanny felt, no erection pressed, nor sated. Not one 'no' needed. Not one.

UNIVERSITY OF LOVE pt.1

9: Defloristation

The final term arrived, still living in malodourous squalor, we had a party at our shitty house, which we'd prepared for by turning off the lights and turning up the music. I'm not much of a dancer, but was having a go, elbows jabbing this way and that, grooving to jazz funk fusion in my golden cigarette-packet hat.

Blotto, a girl grabbed my arm, dragged me to my rotting room and deflowered me. Scant memories include her fragrant hair in my face, the realisation that my only mix tape was extremely depressing, one long feeling of acute naked smelly shame, and a final vision of agonising pain, as of foxes shrieking in the yard.

A new dawn.

I awoke hungover, recoiling cerebrally in expectation of some divine vengeance, initially mortified for having directly violated God's will. I wondered in which way the world had now changed. Could people still see me? I hadn't yet any proof. In anticipation that I'd died, finally, I got out of bed just to make sure my body wasn't lying there motionless, remaining nervous that time itself had stood still, this room my personalised hell, I awaited angels to send me on a quest of retribution. She stirred, at least she is in this new world with me. Maybe it's just us now. Sinners.

Door, hallway, all still there, nervous trip to the toilet, also still there, then back into bed to cogitate in fresh pants. As hours passed, nothing, or nothing else, other than a throbbing member, and a desperate replaying and patching together of fuzzy events.

People started banging about in the house. Reality continued. No thunderclap. No great fanfare. No displacement into a lonely universe. As I stared at the window, a flash of righteous fury overcame all else, stayed for a long while, and then subsided. Slowly, the heavy chains of ignominy fell from my shoulders.

By the time we got out of bed, childhood had become today's chip wrapper. Gravity had stopped working. She was smiling, laughing, and didn't hate me. Oh, happy day. Rife was bliss.

I got overly keen and she snubbed me cold. For a few days my compunction sprung forth romantically under her window, until I saw a naked boy and ran away. Back in my shell was where I felt safest anyway. Dreams an odd lot, nightmares went crazy.

Life was bris. The fiery sensation below quickly developed into a volcano of intense pain, even in the loosest of cotton shorts. Elasticated underpants an absolute impossibility. It so materialised that *mutinium extremis* had been somewhat badly damaged in the scuffle. Maybe heavenly reckoning *was* due after all. Instant moral karma; nob-caned by a phallocentric divinity. I felt quite certain that God must be in the process of marking me impure with a deadly flesh-eating disease, one that would spread across the entire body intensely painful inch at a time, starting on the fore of phimotic foreskin, which burned to the tiniest touch, as dipped in chilli-oil, lavatory visits a most unpleasant surprise.

Time passed. Healing began, a mere flesh wound after all. Celestial meddling did not, in fact, manifest as a flesh-eating bug. Physically, I would repair, eventually, with balm, a great relief.

Internally, however, it was all kicking off. A life of fuming abstinence befouled of eternal perfection with my estranged gilt-edged girlfriend, for one short painful drunken experience and rejection, followed by a short painful penis, no erection. More distant from humanity than ever, this was not what I'd had in mind when I'd wished a 'sharing of love' into being; guilt, shame, physical pain, shimmering with fuck-it once again. In company; chipper, perky, *friendly* even, but, in the first instant alone, jittery, squawky and panic stricken. Everything out there, in its entirety, translated neurologically into how rotten *I* felt, *me*, a conduit for all the foolhardiness of the universe. Not one cell didn't loathe itself upon waking, surviving and passing out.

Unable to hide shame of dishonour, I started to inspect my ethics as one who'd lost his pure heart, as one whose destiny is certain. Hell it is. The futility of fated existence washed over me, as recognition of destiny does. Antagonised to death, and then some ill-described torturous hereafter, forever, until the rapture.

I'd begun to reimagine a one-size-fits-all pain-free afterlife, where ancestors await in full knowledge of shameful thoughts, the orgasm deal cut with God as a child, all of it. At death they'd wind back time and do a walk through, pausing and rewinding at all the bad choices to discuss what could've been done better, sitting through the tedious bits in real time, scrutinising masturbation techniques with a knowing eye, for aeons, and *then* reincarnation, or something. It didn't explain why the ancestors were there in the first place, but better than fire forever, *maybe*.

Divine violence's visceral vermiculation vaguely alleviated by vivisection of vain unheavenly values, how now, indeed, to make henceforward tolerable? If an afterlife reflected one's actions in this life, there'd be solace in integrity. In which case, for a happy ending, I'd have to own up, soon, before I died, it must be the next and last thing to do, a deathbed admission. Lying to myself and my parents, fine, but I couldn't keep lying to the girlfriend.

I called her halls every half-hour until she picked up, but then couldn't find the words. We agreed to meet up when we could.

At year's end, in July, the housemates headed homewards, as time was fit to do so. I stayed in that empty shitty house just as long as I could, hanging on to every blessed uninterrupted minute; sitting, thinking, contemplating, dawn to dusk, for the first time, not *having* to do anything or be anywhere for anyone.

A few good friends remained nearby; we cleared their freezers and watched crap telly in the peace of cynical laughter. The mind inflated like a weather balloon, to the size of a pea, as life's events flashed by for the last time. Contented, done, ready and waiting for death, any, moment, now. Now. Now...

Now now now now now now now now now now now now now
now now now now now now now now now now now now now
now now now now now now now now now now now now now
now now now now now now now now now now now now now
now now now now now now now now now now now now now
now now now now now now now now now now now now now
now now now now now now now now now now now now now
now now now now now now now now now now now now now
now now now now now now now now now now now now now
now now now now now now now now now now now now now
now now now now now now now now now now now now now
now now now now now now now now now now now now now
now now now now now now now now now now now now now
now now now now now now now now now now now now now
now now now now now now now now now now now now now
now now now now now now now now now now now now now
now now now now now now now now now now now now now
now now now now now now now now now now now now now
now now now now now now now now now now now now now
now now now now now now now now now now now now now
now now now now now now now now now now now now now
now now now now now now now now now now now now now
now now now now now now now now now now now now now
now now now now now now now now now now now now now
now now now now now now now now now now now now now
now now now now now now now now now now now now now
now now now now now now now now now now now now now
now now now now now now now now now now now now now
now now now now now now now now now now now now now
now now now now now now now now now now now now now
now now now now now now now now now now now now now
now now now now now now now now now now now now now
now now now now now now now now now now now now now
now now now now now now now now now now now now now
now now now now now now now now now now now now now
now now now now now now now now nooooo oooohh ffuucckk.

UNIVERSITY OF LOVE pt. 1

part 1a

—

Home Groan

UNIVERSITY OF LOVE pt.1

10: Gracelessland

Sussex called. Moving fun. Welcome home. Good to see the family. Shame to *still* be grounded. No cash, no access to cash. Get a job, here, phone, call the club. No, thanks. Why not, *lazy*? Um, er, om. Yellow pages, job agencies, the first A., interview booked, popped on down, promise of a job in a day or two.

Under that roof, I'd amends to make before family bonds could be sutured. I needed to serve my time, follow orders of progressive parental redemption, take their advice without lip, be useful, earn back respect previously lost being the family idiot, their strangely troubled youth needing to be tamed. Jump? Certainly, how high? No booze, no girls. Sure, oh, wait, what?

Home cooking choked in the throat, hard to swallow through a phantom desire for death by emaciation, which I'd hoped to overcome with access to food, but found I still had a real lack of hunger for. Let's say Grace. You know, I've suddenly lost all appetite to survive the day. Laughs couldn't be shared, tension vibrated along taut strings. Expectations of positivity were *so* manically high, as we tried to make the most of our short time together, that any speak of love had me running off for a cry and a rage, pushing blood to the head in silent screams for many many *many* minutes at a time. I guess I'd not really given up on the idea of a brain haemorrhage either. Come back to the table. Nnnnnngh, just a few more minutes, nnnnngh. Nnnnnngh.

By personal choice, and yet, not by choice at all, lost, outcast and living in the wrong universe. I definitely didn't want to be such a little shit, so selfish as to reject lovingly prepared food and exultant talk of their loving God's love, but, while hiding the actual Devil inside, biting Him back, unavoidable reminders, such as prayer, set dying embers ablaze.

Oh, to feel that swim of family love, that spin of joy, when we'd stand together in church to sing lyrics praying for the rapture within 'our generation', and equally doomsaying stuff, happily, blissfully, ignorantly; before doubting a Protestant inheritance, before knowing what it meant to be labled w.a.s.p. as a bad thing by hippies, before querying scripture, which, even in private, still felt horrendous. With each new blasphemy came dizzying episodes, the emotional vertigo of sacrilegious detachment.

There were several lives required, a few just for me, a few for family, a split personality, if you will, as so many of us have, without the need to be diagnosed as having multiple personality disorder. More a multiple personality order than anything.

A dull-eyed soft-spoken hipster, the main face, got on with day-to-day activities by autosuggestion and self-hypnosis. Duh.

A kind child would allow mention of Jesus' infinite love without smashing things, crushing down any disagreements into a singularity never to be dealt with in polite company. Om.

An old sceptic, taking notes; applying amateur scientific rigour to statements of scripture; storing questions to return to later when enjoying actual freedoms, away from religious absolutism pouring salt on all-purpose ethical cultivations; disdainfully taking scissors to the instruction manual of an amoral racist God one unnecessarily misleading statement at a time. Hmmmmm.

An erratic personality ranted, raved, ransacked rooms and struck rock hard walls in morbid self-awareness of stupidity, and in disbelief of such a widespread collective idiocy. Grrrrr.

Another squealy brain-squeezer would run away to cry. Wah.

Another would get any unwanted fatty food back up. Bleh.

Many more fragile states of mind delicately juggled, as is normal, all victims, all children, all grown-ups, all upset and anxious, all wishing for just enough faith to believe so as to be able to ignore restrictions in the physical world and revel in googoo-gaagaa blup blup bang shooey as the truly religious do.

Unhappily, no faith could be found, I wasn't in the business of giving up my new set of partial-liberal-worldly-truths only to faithfully return to the more familiar sets of known lies, for there were one or two difficult 'facts' that superseded all pertinent religious exceptionism. Upon this topic, my minds were as one, one big mess, a contrarian teenager, splintered into fragments, living a shocker, needful of love, knowledge, a sulk, and therapy.

The ban on criticising religions and the religious stood as law, *especially* in that house, but widely too. I couldn't help but think that religious recrimination and a few home truths would be just what billions of sensitive idiots, such as myself, required.

Surely, any good Protestant should protest? Yes? Yes. But, no. Not me. Not to the parents. I yearned to tell them that their God's blessings weren't all they'd claimed them to be, yet, mind-knotted, kept most of the biggest questions to myself.

So, if 'our' 'Lord' is so loving, and we're going to talk of 'Him' as the Holy Trinity, 'Them' no less; where were 'They' when I had a dick up my arse? Was I touched by the hand of the Lord Himself? Was it a transubstantiation of Holy Spirit that I wiped off my leg? What *purpose* has a Being, who receives thanks for intervening, but never intervenes? Superior moral guidance? Since when? Gay rights? Ah, Jesus Christ Emmanuel. Child abuse? Ah, Lordy. Why am *I*, of all people, more accepting of homosexuals than the scriptures? Fundamentally, all religions start with scripture, scripture is homophobic, factually, so, in a world of equitable equality, aren't Liberal Christians a paradox by very definition? Isn't 'personalised-religion' a failure to observe 'Holy-decree'? Feminism: or, an unknowable, ineffably homophobic God? Either: one, or the other, is that really a life choice? Seriously? How to reveal the mind of such a God? Exorcism? Would one need to be a vicar? An atheist? Both? Is it legal to renounce a family Church publicly? Refute a God-given heritage? Is it *illegal?*

Moot muted contentions.

Asking for a friend, I set up some moral mysteries for the parents to tackle, much in the manner of the vicarious victims I so reviled, to allow opportunity for the best of their thoughts to be given a fair airing, that I may glean the right kind of advice. We discussed the carefully chosen subjects cagily, until clichéd logic bubbles popped out. I remember most: forgive and forget.

Forgive and *forget*. I shall *never* forget that, *unforgivable*.

Forget? Fuck off. Things need remembering, not forgetting. It's entirely backward and inverted. Shall we forget our lessons? Our growth? Our scars? What'd be the point of learning *then?* What would be the point of anything if, as soon as it happened, we went out of our way to wipe it completely from our minds? Lest we forget, wars, what are they good for? Remembering. Not to glorify, but as a reminder that we shouldn't go down that terrible path again. Active forgetting? Not the greatest advice. But where *is* the good advice? Which sacred words hold 'truth'? In a sprouting intellect it isn't feasible that one *could* know what to forget when so much is learnt from studying peripheral facts, then altering, adapting and supplanting the slew of new pieces onto muddled or empty mind-maps. Here be dragons. Forget all, but for that which we instruct you; don't just hide your light under a bushel, put *your* light out, take *our* light, spread *our* light. Here be goldfish happinesses and ingrained parrot effluent. Without a reliable cross-cultural guidebook, interpreting the conflicting truth claims is an impossibility, as is the case with; science and religion, secularism and religion, law and religion, capitalism and religion, communism and religion, literature and religion, every 'true' religion and any single 'true' religion. *Forgetting* rival truth claims reinforces mythical beliefs: mythiefs, if you will. I wasn't gonna have my experience stolen from me. Besides, to preserve my own various sets of lies, I needed to remember everything, *every* little thing, every single tiny little bloody thing, sharply, acutely, microscopically, by necessity.

Forgive? Koff. Oh to be of such a skywards state of mind, so elevated, so freely able to take laws unto oneself to pronounce judgement upon another's behaviour, or one's own behaviour. Oho, here we go, I'm forgiven am I? *Yes, you're forgiven.* Nice, thanks, so, *muggins*, the action that offended enough to merit forgiveness didn't injure sufficiently to form a lasting grudge, great, well, expect those behaviours again, and worse, and soon, as the kind of person who obviously tries to forget things too, you daft *mug*. Forgiveness *too easily given* is a let off. It's not your fault, you're freed from the consequences of your actions, you weren't to blame. That's how all-too-easy forgiveness goes. To *qualify* for *real* forgiveness, from within or without, desire to behave 'better' *than a previous incident* must be shown to be processed, acted upon, and proven over time, and yet, *and yet*, 'f.&f.', frequentative fungible flub, 'f.&*fuckingf.*', for forlorn fools to fuddle and fudge, as fits the foot. Once sound-bitten, twice shy, thrice shite, try *that* for size. Turn the other cheek? Are you mad? Terrible advice. Sadist advice. A tooth for a tooth, is a valid truth too, let's have a piece of *that* action, I'll bring the broom handle. Is forgiveness to be forced upon me and mine, due to family claims that the justice of the NT supersedes the justice of the OT? Am *I* a mug? Are my *family* mugs? Are *all* good Christians mugs? How does one find out? Who speaks for Christians? *God*? Yes? Through scripture, directly? No? Through just the one church? No? Only prayer, directly? Oh. Then, are *you* a channel to God? Are *we*? Are *they*? Are *your enemies*? Do *we all* speak for God? Just those representatives that *you* agree with *currently*? Really? Reheheheally?

Well, fine, if forgiveness is more important to our society than retaliation, that we may continue forgetting those in our midst who quite literally need to be educated in right and wrong, fated as creed instructs, here's my cheek, jutting, proudly defiant, sucked up and stuck out, ready for someone to knock out a truth.

Whatever it is that troubles you, Jesus washes away your sins, but wherever He'd washed mine, I wanted them back. I needed to suffer, wallow, sift through my 'sins', to separate right from wrong, compare and contrast, dissect, scrutinise, understand mistakes with no excuses, no demons to take the fall, no unseen forgiveness thrust upon anyone, for *any* reason, ideally. When the claim to moral authority is exigent upon an unprovable mind in Man's invisible image, such an act of hubris, as to forgive on God's behalf, is no more than an empty decree, a public shaming delivered by an arbitrary community of localised curtain-twitchers.

A-whirled of indifference, with a yes-yes mentality of regret, as from one who owed, and will forever owe, a debt of life itself to the parents, I found myself sat on their floral-patterned couch, saddened, confused, envious of their easy love, mulling the tree of knowledge of good and evil, godly lies and serpentine truths, slow-stirring over-emotionalism to calm, thick, brain-custard, unable to remove the frown from a fretful face for family photos as famous effing phrases fermented and fomented fruitlessly, fundamentally fully-unenlightened in a world of difference.

Obliged of love, food, roof, bed, I still didn't want anyone's haughty damn forgiveness, and yet, and yet, they *were* correct, f.&f. happens naturally in a tired brain. One simply cannot maintain a pure concentration of hatred at all times of the day and night, if, say, blood sugar is low, or if, half of the time, problems remain unspoken behind other insignificant issues.

There were only a few people who I felt truly superior to. Fuckers. Ironically, they were the only people in the universe capable of having my forgiveness thrust upon them, and so they got it, they actually got it, or something that felt very much like it, as a part of humanity, part of a hierarchy of decency, an end link added to the chain of common courtesy. *You're* better than *me*; more knowledgable, wiser, but *I'm* better than *them*, *they're* scum, and they'll have to live with that forever and ever. Amen.

A handful of moral high ground still existed below, if I hauled up my mass and squeezed their vile spirits into the infinitely thin crush above rock bottom. In dreamscape's rush, they fell at terminal velocity within my inertial reference frame, close enough to swim over and reach out to slap and punch their hideous daemonic faces in frenzied ferocity, to kick their slain corpses into the horizon of a super-massive black hole.

Wrestling blankets, I'd awake exhausted, allow fury to flourish physically on the alarm clock, take a brief moment for a few deep lungsful of reality, take stock of who I'd be lying to today, then, newly reminded of which threads of sanity to cling to, cool, slowly, to keep the silent peace, such as it was, and wasn't.

Deceptions *had* to endure to avoid upheaval, but those days did not pass quickly, acting the act of false penitence: fenitence, if you will; eagerly enduring the disciplines of the wrong behavioural issues' needless correction, in the wrong person.

Vengeful hush was a bullet in the foot, for having 'forgiven' my trespassers, taking the law into my own hands, judgement away from family, friends, police, and courts of justice, I'd given up on all protections the country could provide, and yet could never provide if I wouldn't testify. And I wouldn't, as Jesus wouldn't. Whilst *not* being crucified to painful death for the sins of strangers, at least, I'd still accepted the sovereignty of *all* sinners, as Jesus had taught, as couldn't be unthought. *My* secret, *my* path to piety, *my* hidden power, *my* victimhood, *my* solipsism, *my* myopia, *my* blindness to public responsibility. Mine. All mine. Ahaha.

Fearful that a fierce fenitent duty too far might finally force fate's hand to defy insufferable fortune and finger the fuckers; wilfully finish foe's futures; it crossed my mind, maliciously, that the act of 'retrieving the soap' mightn't be so much a horrifying ordeal, as a busman's holiday. Contemptible, hateful, but solace, of a sort, backing my inaction with rationale found slithering cowardly 'neath obelisks of forced faux-forgiveness.

And so, sordid lies continued, and continued, and continued, and continued, and carried on, and on; the guilt, false guilt: fuilt, if you will, the fenitence and follity also. Having it both ways, all ways, every way. Controlled chaos, but without any control.

The mind needed to be trained away from holes of thought, but reminders attacked from everywhere. Adverts, for example, in liberal England, don't have women's nipples in them, yet plenty of topless men. It is only a short paranoid hop to thinking the world is set up purely for the satisfaction and sexual gratification of straight women and gay men, and another short hop to feel resentful about it. Oh, the irony. Naked men, persistent as a traumatic image on the retinas, a subjective set of abhorrent images to trigger morose antagonism: mantagonism, if you will. I didn't want to see topless men's nipples on adverts, or album covers, or packaging, or men, or me, or anywhere at all, public places generally, the very sight taking resentful thoughts down the slippery slides to recall and rumination of dark matters, staring at eternity through any cosmos getting in the way. Immediate, intense flashbacks of flesh violation, sympathetic pains not uncommon, in some circumstances there is no choice but to curse and shake helpless fists at the sky. Constipation, for instance, torment. A life sentence, unable to clench buttocks around a hard stool without creeping shadows darkening an already strained mood.

Drawing up blueprints for magnificent escape, it had crossed my half empty glass darkly that I might want to take someone down with me when I go. Yikes. That's not a path to inner peace. *That's* downright evil. The repaired bootstraps that I'd been tugging so hard at had begun to give out weakly at the eyelets. Poor little old me. Woeful, beyond description or prescription. Drowned in tearful pity puddles, despair smothered each and every spare unmedicated juddering shuddering split-second. Better bootstraps required, but, *still*, it was good to be home.

11: Heartbreak Hole

So where *was* my girlfriend? Next time we were to speak
face-to-face, in *any* circumstance, I'd tell her the explicit truth
about stuff, *all* of it, the complete package, as practiced on so
many pained nights. Apparently, I needed her to forgive *me*
my trespass of adultery against *her*, if we could only talk it out.

Well, once I'd promised my parents that I wasn't going to
meet up with her, I got approval to use the landline to phone her.
I managed to ascertain that she'd moved out of her halls, so
stopped calling there. I phoned her parents house, hoping that's
where she'd be, only to find out that she'd decided to stay in
Scotland for the summer, working through, independent, far far
far away. This devastating news, funnily enough, combined with
house rules, trickled like water off of a duck's back, into a gaping
hole. Her parents said that they didn't know her new number,
which I didn't believe. By the third or fourth time pushing for it
they stopped answering calls, instinctively protecting their
little girl from the madness of a legally proven idiot. I only want
to split up, you'd never have to see me again, don't you *get* it!?
No, they didn't *get* 'it', but, ready to pop, I wasn't going to be
splurging my troubles to her parents *first*, not for access to a
useless phone number; not after so long waiting to have that
heart-to-heart with my loved love, only to waste it on *them*.

The option to speak face-to-face had been taken away, so,
one might think that *that* solves *that*, yes? Yes. But, no no no no
fucking no, it seemed we were destined to be together forever,
only, distant, and entirely uncontactable. I couldn't take any more
shite, I was full.   Decided, once again, but with zero doubts,
though I couldn't tell her, or even leave a message, it was over.
It was all over. Done. Dusted. God would have to bloody tell her.

UNIVERSITY OF LOVE   pt.1

12: Working it out

I don't have a problem, I don't have a problem, *really* I don't. Caught in loops of dumb thought-bottling and panicky defeatism I'd settled back into drinking any booze I could lay my hands on, against the rules. There was never quite enough in the room to satisfy the desire to be slightly drunker than this. Sadly, alcoholism comes at a steep price: the very real cost of money.

The rules stipulated that to leave the house alone, there must always be work booked to go to. So, I worked where I could, and always insisted on walking myself home. Slip, slip away. Sip, sip, hooray. And rum for luck. Pip pip, can't stay.

For cash, evenings passed in theatre pits playing the double-bass for amateur-dramatic shows that previous connections had got me in on. These shows weren't good earners, running for a week or two, paying roughly for themselves in terms of nightly interval drinks, and after-show drinks, and pre-show drinks.

Daytimes were spent at the whim of the alphabetically blessed job-agency, with the tanned beauty behind the desk whose heady perfume melted any full-blooded male into their chair. If there *were* any work, they'd call early on the landline, the other end of the house. Keen to get out, I'd sleep on the stairs near the telephone in hope of leaving the close confines of the big airy house in hope of booze. Financially, they promised more than a pint an hour; I kept an eye on the clock, counting the minutes, licking salty lips, mentally measuring volumes.

They found work sweeping the town rubbish-tip, which I loved, pushing the broom up and down, getting the place clean, poking around in the mucky brass for little gems and keepsakes. I found a working cornet and a snare drum that needed new lugs, but, bottom of the pecking order, the foreman took them home.

They found work in a laundry, folding wet sheets on the sheet-drying-and-folding-machine, with a clicker to count how many sheets had been folded, easy. It wasn't hard to beat the numbers daily, causing irritation and resentment in the lazy mentally deficient foremen. A tiny cold-war was fought. Bye.

They found work adding cod-fat to pork shoulders for Christmas hams, which was fine, as one of few English speakers relaying the foreman's requests by first action, proudly was I given charge of the electric pallet mover, which I managed to reverse into myself, crushing my knee. I never told anyone, but confirmed myself to be a pillock. A lop-sided limping pillock.

They found work kitchen-portering in a chain-store café, which was brilliant, alone with thoughts needing to be thought, ensuring every single little thing in the entire place had been steam-washed, which is great for metal teapots and ceramics, but awful for raw fingertips weeping into communal marigolds.

They found work on the bin lorries, which is hard work, very *very* hard work, punctuated with two hours doing nothing travelling to, and from, the landfill, drinking booze and swearing.

Day one, sent home to get better footwear. Footwear bought.

Day two, survived, hard graft achieved with positive attitude.

Day three, weak chest had frozen solid, back too, I couldn't roll over, cramps in every appendage, bed-agony the only option.

Day four, the pain changed, worsened, bed rest continued.

Day five, protesting physical work at the agency office, the chair-melter wouldn't offer anything else if I wouldn't complete their contracts seriously, so, I did a few push-ups and went back to the bins on a fitness tip, but lasted only a few days. Powdered rubber gloves reacted with open blisters, pulled muscles from palms to chin to ankles sending shockwaves up nerves on touch, broken glass scratching gouges through trousers, spray in mouth, feverish infection, ache without respite was too much, I broke.

Right. Okay. Decision time. Death, or better life? Which is it?

After all things, tax-payers were funding my training as a double-bass player, it would be no more than a direct insult to every hard-working person in the country if I continued purposefully damaging hands and body for a few measly quid, having been given such a glorious opportunity to raise expectations through completing a good education, or near enough, on paper, at least.

Following the principle that if you *demand* better for yourself, you'll get better, I *insisted* on some less-physical work from the agency, overcoming her exotic love-potion with teenage gusto, at which, they immediately didn't find any work for a dry week.

Eventually, they found work as a barman in a *fairly* swanky hotel, when, after a few hours of happy polishing on best behaviour in a black bowtie, a large bearded bully sacked me for wearing a 'scruffy' cotton shirt. He let slip how much the hotel paid the agency for staff at the top of his booming voice, I let slip my hourly rate in reedy self-pitying tones; his thundercloud stopped flashing, slowed its broiling, then dissipated, slightly.

The agency was taking eighty percent. Eighty. *Eighty* percent. Let me repeat that: eighty. The agency were *knowingly* taking eighty percent. *Before* tax. A major shock to us both. We stood blinking for one and two and three and four and five and six and seven and eight and nine and ten and eleven and twelve and thirteen and fourteen and fifteen and sixteen and seventeen and eighteen and nineteen and twenty, about twenty one seconds, speaking volumes with eyebrows and the occasional glottal stop, then stormed off furiously in opposite directions, I, as was my wont, sneakily stopping somewhere secret on the journey home for a swift and soothing snifter.

I stopped working for the agency, bunch of crooks, instead, continued playing bass at the theatres and, in the last weeks of the holiday, painted the car port, for my father, for hard cash; the paint brush like sharp lava in the paw. The short sober walk to the bedroom allowing for zero sneaky alcohol whatsoever.

UNIVERSITY OF LOVE pt.1

13: Brewer's Droop

At the very end of the holiday there was a get together for old tertiary college friends, a birthday or something. I worked hard for permission, then took the train, early, cost be damned.

A crowd appeared. We drank and drank, and we didn't care. Old friends sat around chewing the fat, pondering those who couldn't make it, loved ones lost, like attending a funeral wake, but with the debatable reprieve of not being an actual corpse.

People dribbled home slowly as last trains came and went. Personally, I was so contentedly out of it, so glad to spend a night away from sobering restrictions that I'd made quiet plans to out-party everyone, be the very last one sat on the bench outside the kebab shop, and then go from there. Or stay there.

At the very end of the night, one other, a girl, had also out-lasted everyone and there we were, sat on the bench in a happy silence staring at the greasy people. She: a playmate in orchestras, a stunner, flowers in the hair, surfer chick cool. We'd flirted before, doing bad capoeira in sunny fields. She held my arm warmly; I started crying uncontrollably, again, a passionately sad drunk.

Against my better judgement, I stood up, ranting and raving about the stresses of life, the constraints imposed upon us all, how simple it would be if we all gave up vain hopes of ambition and lowered our expectations to a point that the inefficiencies of a musician would become valued more highly, and similar. Animated, gesticulating wildly, tears rolling chin-wards, arms swinging madly, lips proposing that I'd give it all up tomorrow if it meant a guaranteed future with happiness at the end of it, oh, that it were ever so simply done! When, suddenly, she jumped up, grabbed me, kissed me, and said, breathlessly, that I would be sleeping with her that night. Er, okey-doke.

We walked off with some difficulty, staggering down the hill hugging, kissing, and really getting into it. She grabbed my arse, I grabbed hers and recoiled, she laughed and pushed back roughly; bracing me against walls, lifting a leg between mine with an anatomist's knowledge and succubus' intent. Truly marvellous.

A fitness fanatic, her body hardened by energetic activity, keen on bear hugs, she squeezed out more chemical electricity in those blessed minutes than in a frustrated lifetime before.

God owed me this. All I'd ever desired was this unbridled permission to hold and connect, it could all be so very simple. Life seemed so abundantly vibrant, my pathway had become so perfectly well-defined. I needed this woman in my life.

Unyielding from the moment we'd first kissed, I stood at full salute as we stumbled into her place. We had to be quiet. Really quiet. Accidentally bumping into walls and knocking over vases, catching on the steep stairs, we made it to her loft after much stifled laughter and frolics, then spent a few minutes on top of each other, rubbing, squirming and intertwining, quivering with sexual expectation. We started undressing each other, desperate to be naked, pulling at difficult buttons, straps, toggles, clips and mechanisms. The shorts were off in a second. Shorts. Yeah.

She went to do something important briefly then returned to jump my bones but, in those few short minutes, the beer had come back to bite me, and her. She fell on the floor in a crumpled heap more than once, simply from perching without a sturdy pole to stabilise herself. We laughed and shushed and laughed some more, but my little man had given up and there was no reviving him. *She* persevered, which filled me with impotent glee and haunting visions of perfect failure forever, but when I suggested that, for the sake of further embarrassment, we have another go in the morning, she kindly agreed. Lying side by side, we drifted off into smiley sleeps the both of us, spooning tightly, I, defiantly cupping an athletic breast and most exquisite nipple.

In the morning, a single crusted eye peeled open to take stock of the day. She: as naked as a flame. Gorgeous. Stunning. Superb. I'd never seen such athletic perfection in my brief, closeted life; I smiled and stirred under the bed-sheet with pure chemical readiness within, blood-flow surging through youthful loins.

In the soft gooey viscosity of morning syrup, fortified by togetherness, where doubt and worries had been, strength itself stood glowing. King and Queen of all we surveyed, lustrous imaginings lifted our spirits up into the sky; floating, up up up, led by wanton desire, enwrapped in warm cotton-wool clouds we drifted across the fluffy dreamy effulgence of a viridescent mountain kingdom to the open balcony of a tall fairytale tower, light stone walls, amber lit in burnished pastel hues of dawn, ringed by suits of ancient armour that crumbled at a glance; an imposing four-poster bed, slung satin, crisp linen, rose petals, touching each other in roiling perfection of romantic unity, combined adoration, heart's intent pushed into every capillary, orgasmic to the touch, squidgy tentacle tessellations thrubbed pulses of interdimensionality from jelly neck to diamond-tipped phallus, to belly, to brain, to balls, skin prickling with delight, every smile a great wash of joy, turned inside out and tickled with feathers by a teddy in a dress, alone together, soaring high over twinkling landscapes, up up up, accelerating, up up up, into cold thin air, up up up, silk sheets buffeting in our wake.

Up up up, I gotta go. *Uh?* Wake up sleepyhead, I let you sleep, but now I gotta go. *Wha'?* I gotta go, you gotta go, we gotta go. *Oh*, googoo, c'mere f'ra shnurgleurglemmhmmm. No, now.

A repeeled eye took in her clothed form, dressed to the nines. Glorious. But what was that you were saying? *Whatever* it was, she needed to leave, with barely enough time to grab the shorts from the floor and take a push in the back out of the front door.

We were walking in different directions; I went and got a train. On the train, I realised that I didn't have her phone number.

UNIVERSITY OF LOVE   pt.1

University of Love
part 2

Proem: Carry On Crowing

Dearest beloved family, plodding along together, inadvertently at war with a teenage shitcunt; mission objective: moral combat; everyone everywhere everywhen every which way, to the death.

Divisions deeply entrenched, barracked, sand-bagged; shelled heavily behind muddy faggot-clad walls, mortars of wide calibre. Infantry poised, scanning for potential dangers; itchy-triggered regulars squint out at snipers, prepped to scramble at first word; ready to rush right over the top at a single moment's notice. Go, go go go go go. Head-quarters under assault. Chaaaaarge.

No man's land, where God's reign.

Advancing on enemy territory across sanguine battlegrounds, convoys snake insubstantial supply-chains to the active front. Field-marshal Commander Shitcunt heading up the assault, armed with only an unsharpened ass-jaw. All eyes front boys, rapiers at the ready. Head down, private. Private! I said, *private!*

Mountainous molehills steamrollered flat, frailest innocence beaten back in brutish barrages of blaring bugles'n'brimstone, evermore offensive detachments brawling fiercely one atop the other in high-explosive hard-pounding open bloody warfare.

Under fire, over ice; skating pot-holes, snagged by barbed-wire, howitzers blazing: troops diving blindly into mined puddles to escape cloying onion-gas clouds.   B   o   o   o   o   m   .

Clocked; stoppered. One imperfect moment, extended forever. Kept calm as carrion; remains lying rampant in a knotted thicket.

Ammunition spent, only: The Big Red Shiny Button remained; *that* Big Red Shiny Button, to launch weapons of such immense destructive power that to ever press it, even once, would mean the complete'n'utter annihilation of the entire known world.

Do it. Let's do it. I'm gonna do it. We're gonna do it. Tick.

Prologue: Unenlightenment

Do you swear on the Bible? Do I? Hmmmmm. Well, yeroner, *sure, I* do, *I'm* just a kid; *I* couldn't prove the gospels weren't, well, *gospel,* not on my own; not without checking my sources. Matthew 22v37, Mark 12v30, Luke 2v14, John 21v15-7: God is love *hungry,* we'd got a fair amount in common really. Genesis 1v27. Whoever God *is, was,* and *forever shall be;* however He wrote and edited His works, my *faith* saith: The Bible is God's True Word. Nur. Hebrews 11v1-3.

The revelatory claim is: The Bible *is* God's *final* Word, never to be changed or added to. Revelation 22v18-9. Not to mention paradox duality. Deuteronomy 4v2. Or similar *later* claims. Shhhhh. 2 Timothy 3v12-7. God's scriptural challenge; an inter-dimensional jig-saw without a picture box. Genesis 11v5-8.

Obviously, we cannot *all* be correct, let's just assume that *I* am. Zechariah 8v16. No human being alive would *disbelieve* a family Holy Book. Ephesians 6v1-3. So, neither would I. Amos 3v7.

If one *did* cast doubt upon The Bible, one would be doubting: the nation's belief, The Church, the Right of Kings, Government, Judiciary, Army, Police; the entire edifice would crumble to dust, or not, most likely, but still, rebuilding all of Christendom from scratch was more than I could be bothered to do of an afternoon, so, reluctantly, just let it slide. Proverbs 26v11. God is good *enough,* for me, for now, nnnnngh. John 20v28. Every gap in knowledge, there He was, smeared into cracks. Psalm 119v130. A soft pillow in the face of confusion; a security-blanket in the stove-pipe of doubt; a solid set of well-strapped hob-nailed boots through the undergrowth of primordial cogency. Genesis 6v5. Infinite substance with infinite impossibility. Matthew 19v26. Alpha'n'omega; infinity to the omega power. Revelation 1v8.

And so it is written: God is fully aware of, and *comprehends*, the set-of-all-things-beyond-human-understanding. Acts 15v18. The sum of all unknown knowledge, infinitesimally eroded, as His Big-Plan gets revealed to scientists piecemeal. Proverbs 2v6. Advancement, drip-fed unto us from the flange of the Holy Faucet in a small still voice; equations to sit atop all scientific learning whispered to any listening hard enough. Deuteronomy 13v1-4.

In my young keen heart, scripture subsumed every piece of suspicious new information so that *He* could stake *His* claim to *all* knowledge. Colossians 1v17. The cutting edge of 'discovery' only served to set in stone an unshakeable belief in the made-to-measure, all-inclusive, all-encompassing, one-size-fits-all, supra-mundane, omniscient God of godly forefathers. 1 Timothy 6v20.

The Earth is *billions* of years old... Evolution is a proven *fact*... Hmmmmm, I dunnow, I've been stung before; I'm not *gullible.*

Grab a Bible, open it purely at random, *that's* how it's done; *that's* the best method; *that's* God-given inspiration in action. Genesis 1v24, Psalm 90v4, Hebrews 3v4, 2 Peter 3v8. Phew. Direct to the source for allowable truth claims. Ephesians 2v8.

And so it is, yeroner, when a child of the one true God, having sworn an earnest oath upon scripture, takes to the witness stand with truth in heart to be probed indelicately under spotlight in a hall of strangers, justice falls on blunted sword. Romans 12v19. Once a criminal has, let us say, for the sake of argument, raped, one may assume that Holinesses have been removed from events in this time-line, and so, a swift'n'easy lie from the defendant to contradict'n'embarrass the only existing witness, so as to prevent 'penal' servitude, seems hardly implausible. Proverbs 12v22. Testimony: relying on the honesty of criminals to call a coin-flip by which they then adjudge *themselves* by *their* moral codebook, or whichever book they're working from. Deuteronomy 17v6.

One *true* subjective reality, plus another *true* subjective reality, equals: *one* objectively *false* subjective reality. John 4v37.

As *your* God is my witness, I swear to tell the truth, the whole truth, and nothing but the truth, so help me *your* God, or may He strike me down dead, oh, would you look at that. Mark 3v28. Envious was I; such simple choices within a criminal mind: prison, or perjury'n'freedom; lucky sods, *my* lies just built into more lies, extensively. Romans 7v15. *They* wouldn't even need to lie *themselves*, hiring in *someone else* to lie for them. Jude v4. Yes, yeroner, rape-disease, a terrible affliction, of which my client only recently cognised that he suffered from greatly, having been undergoing great emotional stress at the time. Habakkuk 1v2-4.

Any idiot could see this to be weak foundational bedrock for a comprehensive justice system, one sworn word butting hard up against another; an ethical vacuum between witnesses, where God's very own Royal Sovereign's own Crown Court's own Judges step in to adjudge spheres as circles judgmentally. James 4v12. Bewigged'n'powerful, society carved up thinly as *they* see fit, *their* physiognomy and unknown social exigency phasing in'n'out of favour with the seasons; *their* lofty'n'forthright sentimentality the brass platter upon which justice is served. Ecclesiastes 9v1.

Thus'n'therefore, if it wasn't The Bible, if the justice system used any other Holy, unholy, or merely well-respected book; *or* they had virgins cut up a stack of Books to make a Holy Collage, *or* melted down all Books to be turned into a Super-holy Ink, which was used to print up little reminder cards with the legend: 'Don't Be A Dick All Your Life' on both sides, to swear oaths upon, with criminal self-preservations perverting intra-religious logic at the one end, judicial fashions coming'n'going at the other, depending on funding, there'd *still* be no *guarantee* of a victim's status being recognised, *ever;* not by *Holy Decree.* Malachi 2v17.

Given the option to bash one's thick head against a flawed system, or walk away to find an inner peace, rationality stated quite clearly that one shouldn't allow oneself to be beaten down with the stout'n'sturdy stick of injustice twice. 1 Peter 2v19.

Between: distractions, sneaky snifters, and fraught family fibs, I started looking about, across the seas to a wider warring world out *there;* outside the calm seaside town, where the validity of Holy Writ stood for more than the pettiness of a poor little victim who might not win their day in court; where validity of Books defined daily life'n'death struggles for Holy Peoples rubbed up against each other in condomless propagation in every nation. Genesis 6v14: though it remains uncertain if *that* blessing should apply to *my* mongrel bloodline.   Overlapping truths of: Word, sword, gun'n'tank; God's promise to *one,* slapping down *other's* prayers'n'rights to believe God's unbreakable promises to *them.* Deuteronomy 6v13-5, 32v17.   So, whose Holy Promise *is* false? *Somebody's* theology has to be way *way* off.   1 Corinthians 14v23. I hope the missile hits; I hope the missile misses.   Prayers.   Yeah.

How easy to dismiss wish-fulfilment's efficacy with thought, and yet, if one should renounce The Bible as false, even a teeny-weeny tiny bit slightly untrue, *that* would contradict God's Word; *God's Word,* one doesn't do that lightly, *that's* God's Word; *God,* He wouldn't like that much.   Isaiah 13v13.   Nor His committees. Hebrews 10v30.   By *law,* one *mustn't* be seen to cast *any* doubt on Books containing faith beliefs of the majority, or a minority; one *cannot* dispute *any* right to be obviously obliviously wrong, even prescribed enemies.   1 Corinthians 10v29.   Scale up that insulated individual impotence to a globalised multi-faith world and one cannot shuffle forward for eggshells.   Matthew 10v34.

The claim is that if every hour of one's life is dedicated to the detailed study of God's Word, closer to one's God shall ye be, forsooth.   Ezra 9v3.   To this end, one is told by the most diligently earnest of religious peoples that one *must* learn'n'understand: Greek, Aramaic, Latin, Hebrew, Arabic, Egyptian, Akkadian, Norse, etc., in the ancient form, or remain ignorant of the true meaning of God's untainted unmistranslated perfect Holy Word as delivered to His Scribes directly, or edited later, or whatever.

Language paved the zig-zag Biblical Pathway to Holiness; oh, how I wished to have been born foreign, to have had an easier route to His: Truly True Truths of Truthfulness, laid out by the dice of birth; die of birth? Language hard. Proverbs 18v18. But, running with the idea that Holy Verses become less Holy in local dialects through *mis*translation, *mis*quotation, historic *slant,* etc.; allowing the claim that nearly all of the world's populace have been, and are still, denied access to 'The' Truly True Truths of Truthfulness, to then go on to claim that there could be *'no'* Truly True Truths of Truthfulness available to several billion heuristic mono-linguists is probably pushing it a bit. John 8v32. Couldn't one equally claim that Shakespeare's great works don't translate particularly well into Esperanto? Matthew 16v11-2. One hopes that even a very poor translation would dramatically improve the literary lives of every Esperanto speaker. 1 Hamlet 3v75-80.

Assuming *learning* to be a generally positive experience, and *some* knowledge to be better than *none*, it might be said that popular understanding of Christian Law *improved* with Luther's Deutsche Bibel, of fifteen twenty-two. John 15v22. In English, with the King James' Bible, of sixteen eleven. Psalm 16v11. And when The Catholic Church first moved away from Latin Mass, in The Year Of Our Lord: one-thousand nine-hundred'n'sixty-five, finally giving churchgoers something to chat about besides the bishop's hat. Mark 5v6-19. I hadn't the faith to believe in a God Who'd put His Stamp on His Work, only to then immediately allow it to be translated *badly*, it went against the very nature of the whole Omnipotent-Creator-Judge deal. Genesis-Revelation.

And the Earth is a sphere... Oh yeah, I know *that,* don't tease; isn't it, in fact, an oblate spheroid? More importantly, the vital fact that the heliocentric model was first written down in foreign, *incompletely, after* the Bible, *against* the teachings of The Church, *doesn't, cannot, will not* prevent TTTofT from surviving the misadventure of translation into understanding. 2 Timothy 4v3.

Zealously did I read The Good News from the very beginning until I'd find an awkward bump and skip forward, then the same, bump'n'skip forward, bump'n'skip; skimming for wisdom, ever hopeful that the *next* line would hold all the promised answers; evertheless convinced that the finger-of-God method would be the best route to Truly True Truth, after all. John 20v27-9.

Struggling with Bayesian theology, but with a snarling dogged deism, I begged my parents to stop praying for me, just in case the power'n'purity of their well-intended'n'earnest prayer had summoned'n'sustained a perverse evil spirit, who'd now become entitled to seven generations of our family to persecute cruelly, or whatever. Revelation ch1-22. By intervening in their prayers, my hope was to unbind my soul from a *gambling* God, or Satan, or Whoever it was, is, and always shall be *meddling.* Job ch1-42. Seemingly, a wrathful, vindictive, jealous, petty'n'poetic God. Wait, what? Sorry, what? What's that? Poetry? Job: is: *poetry? Poetry? Poetry* shouldn't be part of God's instruction manual. Poetry! *Poetry! Oh no, not Job!* So, what else is *Holy Poetry?*

As a matter of opinion, subjected to peer review, *my* God's verbose'n'waffly yet succinct'n'pithy Word appeared, at *best,* contradictory, and, at *worst,* murderous. Exodus 20v13, 32v25-9. Slavery, justified as *of its time* in God's Holy Olde Worlde, but no, either it's right or it's not. Exodus 21v20-1. I'd say not, therefore it *could* be irreverently reasoned that I, *sinner,* might still be living, technically, to a stricter ethical code than my own almighty God. Having asserted zero slavery as the only standard worth aspiring to, *all* thinking people demand higher moral standards than The Bible, so, nobody, and surely not *my* God, need waste time discussing the rules for owning people, given that such an act itself is evil. Acts 2v40. And yet, the self-same Holy Book is placed in hotel-rooms'n'court-rooms tax-free, despite explicitly breaking established civil laws. Judges 6v29. Zealots live above *one* set of laws, so, which? Ecclesiastes 1v9.

Gender equality, either it's right or it's not. 1 Timothy 2v12.
Feminism, either it's right or it's not.   Ephesians 5v22.
Homosexuality, either it's right or it's not.   Romans 1v27.
Homosexual murder, either it's right or it's not. Leviticus 20v13.
Thought crime, either it's right or it's not.   Matthew 5v28.
Masochism, either it's right or it's not. Luke 6v26, 1 Peter 2v18.
Progress, either it's right or it's not.   1 Corinthians 13v11-3.
Incestual rape, either it's right or it's not.   Genesis 19v36.
Sacrificing a child, either it's right or it's not. Judges 11v31-40.
Infanticide generally, either it's right or it's not. Psalm 137v9.
Chopping up a gang-raped girl, then dumping her body at sea as
if nothing happened, either it's right or it's not. Judges 19v22-30.
Genocide, of all things, either it's right or it's not. 1 Samuel 15v3.
Cannibalism, for Heaven's sake!   2 Kings 6v28-9, John 6v53.
Bestiality, oh, good, definitely *not* bestiality.   Leviticus 20v15.
Good to stand on some common ground. 2 Chronicles 21v15.

Given the best will in the world; given all the rope available;
given that some stories may be part of a wider learning-scheme
hidden away, when one finds oneself absorbing Biblical Laws
that lay in direct opposition to the statutes of The International
Criminal Court, one might start thinking that God's Instruction
Book would've been easier to follow if His Condemnation had
been future-proofed. Numbers ch23-25. Personally speaking,
I'd long hoped His Advice on genocide, specifically, had been
somewhat more unambiguously dismissive. 2 Peter 1v20-1. But,
but but but but but, the translations are wrong, that's not what
was meant, there's no truth found in misquotation. Exodus 4v10.
Angel interbreeding, either it's real or it's not.   Genesis 6v4.
Smiting people, either it's real or it's not. 1 Chronicles 13v10.
Rising from the dead, either it's real or it's not. John 11v44, etc.
'Leaps of faith' smash up mere 'laws of physics', and vice versa,
and not; *reality* requires no faith, unmiraculously, with its really
really real realism matter-of-factly not unreal. Jeremiah 17v9.

The Word. John 1v1. Larger than entropy data sets; bigger than infinity, all wrapped up in a few square feet of faded text upon incalculably valuable holy-scraps squandered with poetry. *Poetry!* Song of Solomon 1v2, Psalm 59v2, Proverbs 31v6. *Poetry!* If it's all equally *important*, then it's all equally *unimportant*.

Biblical Law, *isn't:* 'The Law'. This should be explained clearly to religious children, and many adults also, to avoid a frustrating lifetime of confused mulling over why some verses seem more Holy than others, which appear to contain the very worst ideas to pump into the seething yoof under guise of God-given guidance. Nearing the millennium, as we were, millions of words had been dedicated to every broad subject that one should care to study; ploughing the whereofs'n'wherefores to winkle oblique truths from ethically challenged poetic fabrication had been surpassed as a route to learning, one no longer had the need to search for confounded truths in this confused: Good vs. Evil, Us vs. Them, kind of a way; one could avoid trawling the mind-net through unjustifiable mass-slaughter of ungodly foreign sorts for the purity'n'continuation of a master race by perusing almost any other book instead, maybe even a picture book. Psalm 108v13.

Without one *conclusive* piece of evidence for God's Big Plan, except for *everything in its entirety*, which is a bit of a cop-out, once the educated understood what was going on theologically, *surely* one of His agents would've suggested a neat expurgation of the evil culturally explosive bits, like good literature, however, it *isn't* good literature, it's God's unchanging Word, or, rather, it *is* good literature, it's God's unchanging word. The Bible. Yeah.

How *could* I have told friends that it was *all* true, *so* recently? Mortified. Morbidly mortified. Dreams became spasmodic. But, if *some* of The Bible *could* be perceived as historic literature, shock horror, *then* the confused truths of its component parts would be cast in doubt *viably,* and we'd all have a jolly good laugh about it, and I wouldn't kick myself awake half the night.

The Books of Moses *cannot* be denied, *surely,* except the poetry; Christianity *required* them, and so *acquired* them, then dismissed *some* of them, leaving it unclear which Laws applied to *our* group, to *any* group, and which are plain daft. Leviticus 11v7.

In the Christian circles I spun in, followers of *only* the OT Laws got a backstage pass into NT Heaven, as living proof of the truth of the set up for the punchline: Jehovah *is* God, and vice versa, *someone* didn't receive the memo; *they'll* meet Jesus upon arrival, or not, or whatever, *I'm* no judge. Romans 2v1, Matthew 7v1-3.

Then, outside The Sixty-Six, there's the Orthodox'n'Catholic *extra* books; Tobit, Judith, Maccabees, Esdras: the *banned* books; Enoch, Jasher, Jubilees: the *lost* books; Thomas, Judas, Mary, et al. *My* heritage had spurned *these* scriptures, so that mono-linguistic cretins, like me, shouldn't feel the need to go scrabbling amongst the rubble for gold that isn't there, but, were they actually *Holy? Some* would say so. What made The Sixty-Six *so* Super-Special?

The next rubble piles to sift were *other* Super-Special Books, similarly summarily spurned so that I needn't require study. Twenty lifetimes of learning: The Veda; Avesta; Agamas; Kojiki; Kitáb-i-Aqdas; Tao Te Ching; Kabbalah; BoM; SaH; Dianetics; various: Codices; Sutras; distilled drops of wisdom on rip-off calendars, transcribed'n'mistranslated meticulously; soundbitten snippets crying out for investigation; not to mention: The Qur'an. Shhhhh.

There're *so* many Big Books, a child *must* dismiss *some* of them as of lesser value or the brain would dribble through the ears. Only *false-gods* sprang from sacrilegious pages *never to be read* on pain of profane'n'profound tormented blasphemous double think. Yet, *if* a Book of *true* salvation'n'Heavenly reward *did* exist, it would seem wise to find out more before death, or apocalypse, or whatever. So, which other Book could slot into Bible study without being a heart-attack act of heresy to read one word of, *and* wouldn't try to disprove my current God? Hmmmmm.

Towering above all the other likely options for eternal truth: The Rope of Allah; The Straight Path; the final *finalest* covenant.

It is widely known that within those beautiful covers, in the rhythms'n'rhymes of perfectly composed, perfectly translated, *sûrah*'n'*ayât,* plural claims claim to outclaim the Bible's claims. Calamity!   My mum will not like that, *at all.*   It all sounded *marvellous*, I couldn't wait to learn more; I'd spiritual neediness enough to give The Qur'an a look, briefly, one *cannot* dismiss just *any* Deity's Book, not if salvation'n'Heavenly rewards are real, and maybe they are, one cannot tell before one is dead'n'buried.

Firstly though, if any book existed of sufficient worth to supersede The Bible, it would need to be better than The Bible, comparatively, which shouldn't be difficult; just a few modern-day certainties of international criminal law in need of double checking, then we'll be home'n'dry, in shâ Allah.   With thought, one *has to* dismiss certain bits of The Bible as false, legally, but should one renounce The Qur'an as false, even a teeny-weeny tiny bit slightly untrue, *that* would contradict Allah's Word; *Allah's Word,* one doesn't do that lightly, *that's* Allah's Word; *Allah,* I should've imagined He would be no more happy about it than my own God was, is, and always shall be, f.&e., Amen.

So, once again, relying on the focused spotlight of modern-day internationalised statute-roll; standards that are heavily policed and remain the only yard-stick by which to measure a Holy Book, as before, starting with slavery, either it's right or it's not. Q4a24-5,92. Oh. Q16a75. Oh, ah. Q24a32. Oh no. Q58a4. Oh, bugger. Eugenics, either it's right or it's not. Q8a22,55, Q98a6. Gender equality, either it's right or it's not.   Q2a282, Q4a11, Q16a58, Q24a60, Q33a59, Q37a48-9, Q51a29-30, Q55a56,72-8... Homosexuality, either it's right or it's not. Q7a80-1, Q11a77-80, Q15a67-75, Q21a74, Q26a165-8, Q27a54-6, Q29a28-31, Q37a133-6, Q53a53-5, Q54a33-40... Beating one's wife, either it's right or it's not. Q4a34, Q38a44. Capital punishment, either it's right or it's not. Q8a12-23, Q24a2.

It is particularly tricky to hide *that* stuff as mistranslation. But, but but but but but, okay, well, surely, if the great *Jihâd* is a submission to internal spiritual struggle; lesser *Jihâd* could never be confused for a Holy War against a 'Liberal West', could it? Integration, either it's right or it's not. Q2a221, Q3a73, Q5a51-6...

World domination, either it's right or it's not. Q2a190-3,216, Q3a111,147, Q4a101, Q5a21,111, Q6a155-7, Q7a166-7,182-3, Q8a12-25,39,55,60,65,73-4, Q9a29,36,43-5,57,64-7,107-12,122-3, Q10a70,99-100, Q13a41, Q16a87-90, Q17a58, Q19a39-41, Q21a44-7,95-7,109, Q22a58, Q33a23-4, Q38a2-16, Q40a30-1, Q43a21-5,40-2,55-70,79-80, Q44a7-16, Q45a4-8,20-38, Q48a22-9, Q49a9-10, Q52a42, Q54a42-3... ...Q103a1-3.

Genocide, specifically. Q9a5, Q11a94-5... Q53a50-1... Q89a6-13, Q91a12-5...

Christians, Jews, Polytheists, disbelievers'n'apostates, burning, forever, in fiery torment, either it's right or it's bloody not. Q1a7, Q2a6-20,24,26-8,39,81,85,99,104,114,119,123,126,167,174,217,254, Q3a4,77,85-91,98,102,105-6,116,127,131,141,151,175-8,181,188,196-7, Q4a14,18,30,37,44,55-6,89-91,97,102,115,137-8,140,145,150-1,161,168-9, Q5a6,10,14,29-33,36-7,41,49,51-3,60,72-3,77,80,86,94,115, Q6a15,25-7,30-31, 36,44,47,70,134-5, Q7a9-10,36-41,44-53,147,173, Q8a14,25,36-7,50-2,59, Q9a2-3,17,24,34-5,39,49,52,63,66,68,73-4,79,90,95,101,109,113,128, Q10a2, 4,7-8,15,23,27,39,45-6,50-5,60,88,93-8, Q11a3,8,15-22,26,33,39,48,60,84,93-5, 98-9,102-7,109,113,119, Q12a107,110, Q13a5-6,18,25-7,31-5,42, Q14a2-3, 7,13-7,21-2,27-30,42-4,49-51, Q15a2-3,13-5,43-4,50,63,90-7, Q16a1,25-9,33-4, 55-6,60-3,84-94,104-9,117, Q17a8,10,13-6,18,22,32,39,45-51,54,57,63,72-5,97-8,105, Q18a2,29,49-58,87,100-6, Q19a37-8,59,75,86, Q20a16,48,61,71-4,100-2,124-7,134, Q21a26,29,39-43,98-100, Q22a4,9,11,15,18-22,25,44,51,55,71-2, Q23a23,32,41,56,77, 103-8,117, Q24a14,19,37,39-40,50,57,63, Q25a11-4,18-9,21-3,26-8,34-7,40-2,65-9,77, Q26a6,91-102,135,200-13, Q27a4-5,80-5,90, Q28a40-2,78, Q29a11-3,23,41-3,52-5,68, Q30a10-4,16,34-7,42-5,57-9, Q31a6-7,21,23-4, Q32a12-4,20-2,29, Q33a8,57,64-8,71-3, Q34a5,8,12,29-33,38,42,45-6,51-4, Q35a6-10,14,19-26,36-40,42, Q36a7-11,43-5,59-70, Q37a6-39,54-7,62-8,161-3,174-9, Q38a26-7,55-64,84-8, Q39a7-9,13-6,19,24-32,36-42,46-52,54-60,65-72, Q40a4-7,10-22,27,32-5,39-44,57-63,69-76,83-5, Q41a4-7,16-7,19-28,40-1,43,47-50, Q42a7-8,16-8,20-2,26,29-31,35,40-2,44-7, Q43a36-9,65-6,74-7,83,87-9, Q44a3,40-50,56, Q45a7-11,14-5,21-2,26-9,31-5, Q46a5-6,18-21,31-5, Q47a1,12,15,25-7, Q48a6,13,16-7, Q49a2,11,18, Q50a2-3,11-30, Q51a5-14,59-60, Q52a6-18,27,38,44-7, Q53a31,53-61, Q54a3,6-7,38-40,45-8, Q55a35-45, Q56a1-10,41-56,73,92-5, Q57a13-6,19-20,29, Q58a4-6,8,14,21, Q59a2-4,7,15,17,19-20, Q60a1-3,13, Q61a8, Q62a5-8, Q63a1-11, Q64a5-10, Q65a8-9, Q66a7-9, Q67a6-11, Q68a42-44, Q69a25-41,49-50, Q70a1-3,11-21,42-4, Q71a1,26-8, Q72a15,17,23, Q73a11-8, Q74a8-31,42-8, Q75a31-6, Q76a4,10,31, Q77a1-450,45-9, Q78a21-30,40, Q79a34-9, Q80a40-2, Q81a12-4, Q82a14-9, Q83a7,15-21,34-6, Q84a6,10-2,22-4, Q85a10,12-3,19-20, Q86a9-17, Q87a11-3, Q88a2-7,21-6, Q89a23-6, Q90a19-20, Q91a10-5, Q92a10-7, Q95a7, Q96a6-8,15-8, Q98a6, Q100a11, Q101a8-11, Q102a6-8, Q104a1-9, Q108a3, Q109a1-6, Q111a3-5...

Poetry, it's not right. Q21a5, Q36a69, Q37a36-7, Q52a30, Q69a41.

Paradise lost. Hate in its purest vilest form. I'll say it again. Hate in its purest vilest form. I'll say it again'n'again, and again, and then again. Wishing Hell upon *anybody* is hate in its vilest form. It doesn't matter *which* Hell; Hell is Hell, here'n'hereafter. Earthly Hell is being strapped to a Holy Book providing *detailed* Hell-hereafters for thinking free thoughts; the vilest vile villainy.

Stop me at any point if you think this could be a hate crime, this whole: not-wanting-to-be-cast-into-a-fiery-pit song'n'dance, I wouldn't want to upset anyone by discussing my flayed body burning in torment with only boiling water for refreshment. But, the fact remains that *I* didn't describe how my family will burn, forever, in painful torment, it wasn't me, and yet, there it is, burned into my reticent retinas, and several billion other retinas also, all of my family, all of Christendom, burning in hell-fire, forever, in painful torment, frying in our ever-replenishing fat.

Then which of the Blessings of your Lord will you then deny? *Blessings?* This should be clear to you, if you'll only understand. Understand *what?* Oh Lord, if they but knew. If we knew *what?* Do you not now remember? Remember *what?* We have indeed made plain the signs for people who believe with certainty. Yes, yes you have, *indeed,* a predestined Hell for all of my ancestors. I'm not reading it wrong, that's what it says, so, yeroner, I shan't believe those words neither; the *hubris* required to so *brazenly assume* that: one's: own: God's: Word, is, er, the, um, *only*, erm.

Oh. Ah. Oh. Um. Ah.

Empathy; *shit;* surculose society *will* keep on, persistently.

Books are books. Books are *not* people. People are people. People are *not* books. Books are books, except for Holy Books, they're different, for: what makes a missionary? Why the word: evangelist? What do evangelists evangelise, if *not* God's Word? Where else is God's Word found, except in the pages of His Book? Round'n'round, and round. Books *are* people, Bookish folk like me; I, myself, proof of troglodytion, but proof of Holy Doubt also.

It's not that we Bookish folk really *want* our enemies to burn, forever, in painful torment, but The Good Books we follow say so overtly, proudly; *we* follow The Rules so that *we* won't burn, forever, in painful torment, where the *threat* of pain purposefully fogs the goggles of objective morality with the peril of hate-fueled hell-fire as a thrashing whip. And, if *we* will not accept our hells; if *we* reject it all, *it* is still spread liberally across the street.

Painted into a Holy Corner of Hell; believe in miracles; toe-step hell's-eggs anti-this'n'that-phobia; show bias for one set of beliefs'n'believers, or another, or all, or none. Hateful as Hell is, criticism of Holy hell-fire ain't advised, policed by religious sorts and politically-correct flag-pole jockeys who're condemned to the very same Hell they're quashing discussion of, because *they* don't believe that any rational human could believe any piece of any bit of any part of it, ignoring those deep Holy attachments inspiring both priest'n'beast to literal spiritual imaginings, at *least*. But, but but but but but, there are worse things written in The *Bible*; people don't have as much respect for *any* Book as is claimed; why assume that an *intelligent* human being could take *Holy Words* as any form of literal truth? Get over it already; no one is religious any more. And other effusive scarecrow whataboutery.

Knowing what I knew about myself, it wasn't an *irrational* fear of *other* people believing dubious Holy Ideas from Holy Books; the Good Folks *I* knew could convince themselves of anything, and did. Christians *have* to believe that Jesus *was* resurrected, that Mary Mother *was* pure, and that the apocalypse *is* near, *obviously,* everything in Christianity hinges on that, and a few other crucial bits'n'bobs; consubstantiation arguments still rage; otherwise, the NT is the story of a bloke with views on how best to interpret Jewish politics, which would never be my speciality, especially in a fraught world where one negative word misheard or wrongly inferred is cause enough to be tarred'n'feathered with terms that shut down access to the best God'n'theology debates.

Standing on parents feet, fleeing the nest, 'free' to intermingle with all God's beautiful peoples on the tacet understanding that everyone observe The Golden Rule: or variations on that theme; a shared belief; a Humanist belief, as humanity; an Animist belief, as animals, that deep down we are all made of the same star-stuff; whoever we are, wherever we are, *we'll* look out for each other; side by side, hand in hand, we all stand together, bomb bomb.

There *was* a time, when I could've been convinced to do almost anything in Jesus' name; when I thought I knew how to worship; when I'd raise my hand up high in 'praise' and really *really* mean it; when I believed prayers would come true if I squeezed harder; when I'd flap my tongue and out would come a babble bubble of blatant bollocks, jealously lauded'n'applauded as a step closer to a personal God; when public exorcism had me persuaded of something more than play-acting for catharsis in a safe space; when *I* believed that all non-Christians *deserved* Hell, that all divorcees *deserved* Hell, striking as a fever of justified hatred against all evil doers, for which I apologise, profusely.

So, Holy special pleading is *not* allowed, no more than my own. I *must've* been claiming more than possibly could be known, and if *I'm* in the wrong, a bit, maybe, then so is *everyone,* for it's not the correct state of things to go around with hate'n'pity for entire ethnic groups within one head, or any single societal grouping, *that* is the exact kind-of-a-thing Hippykind has been 'working hard' to get us to give up, only, Holy Books slow open-societies down by tying existentialism to an existence that never existed. Angel interbreeding, either it's a real thing or it's not. Q3a33-4. Smiting people. Q3a65. Raising the dead. Q6a95. Faith. Yeah.

When was the enlightenment again? It was *before now,* right? It couldn't be the only philosophical movement to have been held in the future. How can it have passed me by? And so many of my friends, how did it pass us by? And so many religious people of the world, how did something so very *very* important pass us by?

UNIVERSITY OF LOVE pt.2

part 2

—

Groan Apart

1: Living

Previously walking blindly into a cheap dodgy house-share with many housemates and their many problems, and mine, burrowing parallel holes through hedges of causality; *this* year, expectations had been raised; going out in a blaze of debauchery; love'n'fun; no fear, no regrets, no *additional* regrets. Me. Yeah.

Impertinently, feet stamped, hands a-flap in panic, I'd insisted *loudly* that new accommodations would *have* to be, at the very *very* least, without subjection to the whims of suicidal strangers and their oh so similar issues, and also, as if that wasn't enough, in a building of sufficient luxury that there'd be the option for oxygen to circulate should it ever prove necessary; announcing flatly that the only acceptable options were to be: living alone, (ahaha, ahahaha, ahahahaha, ahahahahaha, oh, you're serious,) or, at worst, a two-person house-share with one trusted friend, *one, maximum:* or, running far away, freed from the constraint of house'n'housemates, added tragically in hope of caring parents taking the bait. Running away wasn't highly likely with a double-bass in tow, but it tugged mercilessly at tight heart-strings describing the possibility with youthful passion, like an arse.

To raise living standards to these stipulations, more funds were needed; more than had ever been planned for or set aside. Problem parents, having not so long ago received governmental bursaries themselves, conceded that whilst I stayed in full-time education they'd have to officially disown me, so that I too may be granted a governmental award, or, by refusing disownership, they'd have to front up to being The Bank of Mum'n'Dad for the foreseeable future, as required of them legally, and so, if their jittery weepy boy needed such comforts as privacy'n'air, then *that's* what their jittery weepy boy would get, whatever the debt.

Counting up trusted friends: one, er, um. *Panic!* No, *all good.* Pilot to the rescue again, clingy wingman saved; he'd found a 'cosy' two-person back-to-back end-of-terrace further down the same hill, away from the college, past the pub at the bottom. Yes, yes yes yes yes, I'm in. *How* much? Er, um. *Panic!* No, *all good.* Begging for the folks to disown me had worked its dark magic.

The house overlooked a popular route to more housing stock; a thin-walled, creaky-floored, one-up-one-down box stack with a poorly converted cock-loft, built cheaply by benefactors to keep factory workers dry, now repurposed by lucky descendants to wring dry parents of the well-to-do, and just-about-well-enough-to-do, by making a phone-call to employ a cleaner, once, annually, in return for making the mortgage payments plus a large chunk. I wasn't paying for it, sure, but, with bank loans for food'n'such, something inside begrudged that the folks had scrimped'n'saved every penny, only to funnel those life-savings directly into a stranger's purse so that *they* may live subsidised, take holidays abroad, buy luxuries *and* food, *and* more houses to rip-off hard-working aspirational parents long into the future, *without labour,* erstwhile raising the costs of *all* housing for everyone to enjoy.

The lesbian living opposite, her house wider by half; her solid floors, full-length bath, large kitchen, spare room, and freedom to add personal touches, upgrade stuff, work on messy art to define herself in her home as an impactful inhabitant of the world etc., was *buying* her place, *freehold,* for less than each *room* in ours could be *borrowed* for. Such a massive mark-up seemed wrong, as it still does, but that's flowing free-market capitalism for you. Bubble bubble. Don't teach a child to fish, catch all of the fish, make fish-paste, sell fish-paste, put up the price of fish-paste.

We organised keys so as to move in just as soon as possible, sneakily claiming to get a head-start on the other students by jumping the Autumn rush for part-time jobs. A very plausible lie, if I do say so myself. *Another* very plausible lie. *Yet* another.

2: Really Living

I returned to Yorkshire thirsty having paid off most of the interest on a maximised overdraft. Loans on their way. Hip, hip-flasks'n'tinnies for now. Long-suffering parents dropped me off at the new place, had a cuppa, stuffed some folding cash into my pockets and then pootled off, postponing their pensions so that they could afford to continue stumping up for the excessive rent that I'd landed on them. And also the sister's rent. As well as their own mortgage, and bills, and food'n'stuff. Thanks, bye.

Freedom. Glorious freedom.

Large sash-windows opened wide, sliding smoothly in their runners as sash-windows bloody well should at *these* prices. Hanging gibbonesque from the frames, I'd poke positivities at passing people who looked like they needed cheering up. For my small part, I'd decided to give society another chance, expand philosophical spheres, breathe cerebrally, tackle inner idiocy. Yay. As long as I'd perish before the rent runs out, painlessly, rock'n'roll young, having done *something* for distant relatives to dig up, I could learn to live with that, maybe, or not, or whatever.

My pilot arrived later the same day, we unpacked the ashtrays and sentimental knick-knackery, smoked a few cigarettes in *our* lounge, got to the local shop for some cans, the local man for a lump, and were doing hot-knives off the electric hob by nightfall. No fan of hot-knives, we hastily assembled a plastic bottle, some flexible plastic tubing, gaffer tape, and a trumpet mouthpiece; bubble bubble. Next, we set up a small b.&w. with a coat-hanger aerial, tuned it in, then settled ourselves into the soft seventies strap-sofas, one small sunken two-seater each. We toasted our excellent fortune, shut the windows, drew the blinds, pulled the curtains, roasted some cigarettes, and boxed ourselves in.

Luxurious private smoking, without threat of reprisal, flowed over the crown like warm treacle. My pilot'n'I were of one mind, we'd made a pact that ours would be a smoker's house; a house of *any* vice, whenever possible. We laughed hard'n'long'n'loudly over the vaguely humorous notion of getting stoned to death.

I loved private smoking. Private smoking turned off the world. Something inside went aaaaah. Aaaaaah, it went.

Aaaaaah.

Knock knock. Hello, come in, oh, *goodnight,* oh. *Clump clump. Thump thump thumpety thump.* We'd agreed that he'd be best in the attic, far away. Regular thumpings couldn't be heard very *very* loudly from the lounge, so I got into the habit of zzzing on the couch near the window, free to do that which came naturally, alone, all night, ever hopeful of a petite fuzzy watershed nipple.

On occasion, I could full body orgasm without touching myself. If tired, a few well-chosen strokes achieved similar results; good times. Left in peace at the very peak of teenage fertility, nature could be answered just as often as she called; wake up, orgasm, smoke, drink, orgasm, smoke, orgasm, drink, smoke, orgasm, maybe eat, maybe sleep, maybe not, and start over.

On a strict budget, only luxuries afforded, I fully embraced the fact that stimulants are more effective on an empty stomach; lows cut so much deeper, highs cut so much shallower. Addicted to strong feelings in any form, love revolved slowly through hate as convictions blossomed into floridly-worded lack of expression, sad'n'happy 'brains' each taking turns to lead the merry dance.

The poisoned knife of anger stabbed at the heart. Better still, with uninterrupted lack of sleep, parabolas of rage-induced feeling exponentiated into sustained psychotic polarisations: mirrored loops of good'n'evil, right'n'wrong, strain'n'collapse; life limitations glimpsed through ever-widening lenses, flipflapflop; completely unable to describe any single piece of any part of it.

Thump thump thumpety thump, thumpety thump thump.

3: Really Really Living

Popular culture hadn't really made an impact before, and now, suddenly, endless television, with a *fifth* nipply channel too; *epic.* Radio Times in hand, couched under duvet in a private haze of heavily tobacconised vapours, plans were laid to press the button to change channel, all the long way over there on the teevee set, past the easily-upturnable coffee-table, and other obstacles.

Thoughts coalesced upon love; my long-estranged girl-friend. Shamefully, appallingly, our relationship lived on, on paper, contractually, yet, I *couldn't* see her, phone her, or send a letter, for her newly updated details escaped me, and I *wouldn't* see her, for motivation to search her out had vanished into smoke.

I loved being in love with her. Loving her turned off the world. Something inside went aaaaah, fuck it. Aaaaaah, fuck it, it went.

Aaaaaah, fuck it.

Eternal commitment filled the empty room with the rotting stink of personal failure. Such a huge gamble for us both: marriage; citizenship; God's blessing; forever missing out on the joys of experimental experiential guilt-free teenage exploits with willing nubile energetic sorts for hour upon thumping hour.

Since asking her out nearly two years earlier, dancing around the pub like a cockney, I'd somehow lost my virginity by accident, *twice,* and hadn't told her about it. *My* lie, to do with as *I* see fit. Nur.

Any future bubble with the two of us living happily together, existed only as a possibility *if* she'd forgive my transgressions thus far, and any more teenage circumstance likely to be thrust. By my own unknown inexact standards, *I* wouldn't forgive *me* for breaking *our* solemn virginal promise and, try as I might, couldn't find a single reason why *she'd* think any differently.

As a wannabe hippy, I'd started to reconsider our relationship as something shameful I'd *'done to her',* had been *'doing* to her', was *still 'doing* to her', trapping her inside controlling behaviours that any decent flower-child should feel ashamed of; ensnaring her, coercing her, baiting her into bonds of marriage that *some* of the world approves of, much of it, *most* of it, but *not* hippies.

Do you? Do I? I do. Or *do* I? Well, I *would,* if we could skip the Heart-break Motel, say our flowery vows in a field under a tree on a sunny day, consummate, to get a feel for it, and *then* wait for youth to evaporate from under us, so *very* many miles apart.

I take thee to be my wedded Wife, to have and to hold from some day forward, for worse, for poorer, in sickness, to love and Chernobyl, till death us do part, or till a better offer on the table us do part, or till parting us do part, according to God's Holy ordinance, and thereto I plight thee my trough. And thus it was, and thus it wasn't. Schröedinger's Catholic. A marriage of super-imposition *and* observable collapse; our subset of universes had been selected and we were headed for destiny. Tick. Tock.

We were both to be getting a whole human-being in the deal, one human each, which, all things being equal, seemed fair, only, unfairly, *hers* would be tarnished, whereas *mine* would be mint. My imperfection wasn't her fault, but that is the way it goes, that's how it is sometimes, luck is luck is luck. I felt sorry for her, for me, for her, for me, for her; I shouldn't be putting *that* on her, nor putting that silent scream of sad'n'mad upon anyone, surely.

Buck-up lad, the shoulder voice chirped in, modern women don't want needy men, no one does; strong, sexy, hippy women rightly say that it's the duty of needy sorts to leave friends and loved ones unburdened; to reject those loved most dearly so that there'll be less chance to burden them heedlessly with needless issues; surrounding oneself with strangers is best, it hurts less long-term. Oh, woe, oh woe, oh won't you just shut up, you silly *silly* little shoulder voice. Only if *you* change channel. Nnnnnngh.

She was perfect. Would an adulterer ever be good enough? No, unless she *wasn't* perfect. Don't think it. Had *she* been faithful? Don't *think* it! Had she been *unfaithful?* Shitballs.

The accusation blew in through the letter-box and lit a match. Oh my God, I blasphemed aloud, my inner Christian momentarily distracted praying fervently that she *had* been faithful and would long remain so. Suddenly serpentine, the shoulder voice wished she *had* shagged someone, selfishly assuaging my adulterous failures. If *she'd* cheated on *me,* equalling *my* drunken snippets, *then* we'd be karmically rebalanced, and I'd get a repaired set of psychological bootstraps *so* strong that I could tug'n'pull my soul back up into that lovey-dovey floaty-gloaty cloud of moral equity.

Highly improbable parallel universes were summoned from the now finite selection in which we'd be karmically equal, but, *horror,* in each universe summoned, it seemed that she *had* to be *at least* as tarnished as I was, mathematically, stroke for stroke, or, *horror of horrors,* she'd *have to be* out shagging currently while I'd be cursing my lot for nothing. Karma didn't redress grievances, it only piled on more. Hmmmmm. In which of these universes am I *not* a massive bastard? I kept sieving, fruitlessly.

Probable paranoia kicked in; as probable as one. One in one. I, myself, mathematical proof of the likeliest statistical outcome. Puritanism hadn't helped *me* escape fate. It seemed certain beyond unreasonable doubt that she, being a teenage puritan too, would fall in love with *her* nearest available heart's desire, get drunk'n'horny at some point, and then do that which hormone-flushed teenagers inevitably tended to do, in one way or another. Unfocused projection, askew, upside-down'n'back-to-front; but, but but but but but I've got an excuse, I'd lie to myself. Foolish, contemptible, hypocritical twat-cockery. Blood on fire, burning, forehead in painful torment; love bends; bubbling underwater without the 'Snorkel of Trust'. I didn't deserve her, or anyone, which was fine, as that's exactly what I'd gone'n'got. *Good.*

Bad. Envy raged against this irrationally invented nemesis, with his perfect incisors, portfolio'n'pension plan; my forever sworn enemy, whose existence I couldn't disprove or stop myself from thinking about. If he *didn't* exist *as yet,* by stepping inside these new universes of certain probable possibility, he *would,* and, once I'd perished, reasonably soon, we would be locked in an eternal struggle to win the right to entangle our dark matter with *her* heavenly soul. I'd jump the punch, somehow passing over to the other side maintaining all the anger'n'spite built-up during the crescendo into heart failure, wait around a while, to spy on them and ruin *his* life as a ghost, then all *eternity* to fight immortal combat to win Heaven's glorious eternal rewards: glory-glory-hallelujah, or gory-gory-Hell-luge-wah. Life is very *very* short, it *feels* long, but it isn't. Eternity, conversely, is very *very* **very** *very* **very** long, and *must* drag on for an immortal soul when fury is the only prescribed activity on the bulletin board. One *must* assume that time becomes a great healer at *some* point.

Though hated, he *could* be a saviour too, *if* I lived that long. He'd pop round the house in lucid dreams and, maybe because he was a known figment of imagination, maybe hoping to learn something about the subconscious brain, I would invite him in, sit him down, make him a cuppa, ask if he *truly* loved her, then kill him, many times, in increasingly inventive'n'nasty ways.

Proud dumb-love or shame, or something, kept broody dreams alive as the price of psychotic hippydom sat heavy upon the ribs. I hated *having to* let her go *because* I loved her; I didn't deserve her, true, but felt conned into giving up that-which-was-most-beloved-in-all-the-world by a crass song-line soundbite taking up a class-action against olde-worlde panoramas; visions of slow-motion frolics in yellow fields, fairies, flowers, cloudless skies, children giggling playfully on summer days with no regrets. Well, no, *some* regrets; imaginary *lovers,* fine; imaginary *children,* normal; imaginary *enemies,* self-abuse of the highest order.

As a man who'd wanted to make a baby with the woman I loved most dearly, I'd had to ask, it would've been rude not to. The outcome of this is to have made historic sexual advances toward a soul possibly destined for another, and she'd said no. There's no denying that she'd said no; no *is* the word she'd said. Before I could ever push that big red shiny button for myself, the expectation fell on *me* to first stick *my* hand in the air, to admit to lustful thoughts, unwanted advances, controlling actions, abusive power-plays, deviant sexual behaviour, inappropriate what's-its, whatever else'n'what not, before God, or St Peter, or whoever.

Hi, can I help? No, just waiting, thanks. Oh, lover or enemy? Er, both. Ah, fighting for entanglement, lovely; Heavenly Arena, through The Gates, up the cloud, seventh on the left, can't miss it. Uh, actually, there's something I ought to do first. Ah, the ghostly revenge package? That's right. Children? What? How many children? Oh, none. Ah, *well,* you can't return without children. Oh, uh, I didn't know it mattered. Of course you did, bloodline is the whole deal. Oh, fair enough, well, I *suppose* it'll be a fight for entanglement then. Ah, entanglement, lovely, so, you have your marriage certificate? Oh, no, we didn't get that far. Oh dear, well, I'm afraid you won't be able to fight for the right to entangle if she *does* marry; is that *likely?* Certain. Oh, ah. We were waiting. Ohoho, surely you're not a *virgin*, I've not seen a fully-grown virgin in years. Um, no, not really. Not really? It's complicated. *Complicated?* I tried *hard*, but not hard enough, or way too hard, I could never tell, I got easily confused by girls. Ah, you're *not* a homosexual, geez, you mustn't be *here*. No, *no*, well, um, no. Oh, really? Really. *Really? Really.* Look, it's totally fine if you *are*, but you shouldn't be *here* in *reception, some* folks still get a bit funny, the Anglican party are through The Gates, down the cloud, seventy-seventh on the left, disco-lights, loud music, can't miss it. Sir, given a choice, I choose death-death, and will accept no other. Sorry, not for *you*, it's *praising* today. And tomorrow I see.

4: Adulterish

Then, a popular princess died, TV news rolling rolling rolling. Rawhide. The footage of her last press conference, where she'd declared tantalisingly to have important news to announce at the *next* press conference at their *next* destination, vanished quickly, it seemed to imply motive for murder; we kept an eye out, but it didn't return. Conspiracy abounded. On every channel, non-stop news-reporters stuck their mics into faces of numpty-muppets who'd never met her, bawling into their red, white'n'blue hankies; sputtering how she'd walked with them on their journey through hard times; what an inspirational figurehead she'd been to them.

Not me. She'd not inspired me. I wouldn't allow the thought to take root. It seemed to *me* that she'd broken her lifelong vows to God, *and* our future King, which is *not* cool, surely. Oh. Ah, shuddup. Things are never that simple, we were then informed: she'd fought bulimia, kissed an AIDS victim, worn khaki near a minefield, taken an interest in: sports, defence, foreign affairs; had a messy divorce; she'd fought tooth'n'nail with The Media that broke her, maybe she *did* define our generation after all.

Since: The Restoration, and even more so: The Television Age, royalty have an *even* greater responsibility to behave 'properly'. Character role-play; which behaviours are correct? Let us look to The Royal Standard, oh. So, if beloved royals can behave 'badly', and still have a nation of twat-muffins waving flags'n'wailing like idiots, then *maybe* adultery was more acceptable than I'd been encouraged to believe in my tiny monochrome world, and *maybe* poly-amorous activity shouldn't be chastised so heavily by a sheltered idealistic teenager. Absolute moral certainty started to look less absolutely absolute as wave after wave of teary-eyed glorification unlocked mind prisons, one little grey cell at a time.

Not being royal, or a likely future royal, nor of the aristocracy, nobility, or upper-classes, while jazzily wasting away the middle-class aspiration of youth, too cash-poor to be a proper hippy but surely not working-class, *God forbid, I* didn't have the eyes of a nation analysing *me*; it wasn't *my* duty to lead by example, but, but but but aaaaah, fuck it. Rolling rolling rolling. Slowly, very *very* slowly, picking through God's Law, visions expanded to take in adultery as a 'tolerable sin', not worth being *actually* killed for.

For a first time locked to a telly, it didn't impress or improve; BBC programming cycled round sadly, a constant morose dirge, both channels identical from: breakfast, until: end of broadcast; the other staticky channels also a morbid national wrist-slitting, although with abnormally long advert-breaks and occasional unscheduled popular shows thrown in entirely unannounced.

It needn't have been this way, a short update every few hours would have been sufficient, to reassure us that she was still dead, just in case she'd risen-again as the deity some impertinently described her as, but no, the anthem blared continually as the tsunami of grief swept across the country. Goooood saaaaave... ...aaaaargh. Why aren't you standing up? Oh, ha ha, like singing the anthem did *her* any good; wah, lets all have a sob, like a candle in a guff of wind, oho, here we go; Goooood saaaaave... ...arse. I wished I'd never bought the bloody Radio Times, it was, after all things, 'The Press' who'd killed her, or so *they* claimed, somewhat tentatively. To engage with any News-Media suddenly felt like state-sponsored terrorism, so we decided, for the best, that we weren't going to pay the TV license if 'they' were going to use it to chase innocent people down to cause sudden violent death. It's only right'n'fair, it's what she would have wanted.

I didn't want to admit or accept that a princess could inspire *me,* not being prone to such things, but she *had*, just a little bit; to *act* upon lascivious intention, because spreading love freely seemed to be of the highest royal virtue, *and* life is fleeting, get on with it.

5: Three Brittle Words

The girl-friend called the house phone, I couldn't draw breath. Hnnnnngh, I spoke meaningfully into the speaker as eloquently as could be mustered. I called your parents, they say phone 'em, are you alright? Uuuuuum. Okay, tell me. Okaaaaay, yeah, um, there are a *few* things. Oh, you haven't got another girl-friend? What, er, no, um, nope, erm, no, nothing *quite* like that, have you? I haven't got a girl-friend, no. *No, a boy-friend?* Alright, *easy,* why so serious? Ahahaha, great joke, have you got a new boy-friend? *What?* Do you fancy anyone? What's all this about? *Tell* me. No, I *haven't,* I *don't.* Okay, well, good, er, well, um, that's, erm, that's alright then. What's *up* with you? Um, oooooh, well, I dunnow: justice, truth, holiness, life, death, the, um, the fact that, erm, that: I love you, for a start. Aaaaaah, I love you too. Good, um, good, er, great, erm, yay, please, tell me your news; tell me everything.

And then, I don't remember much; suggestions of her freedom from my cerebral clutches would have to wait for another day. Happiness flooded the mind with a lightness that lifted the head, straightened the spine, and opened the airways; tingling body-tissue pumped full to bursting with transcendental energies of organic enrichment, enough fuel to keep mind'n'soul happily bubbling for several weeks without need for replenishment.

I love you then. Yeah, love you too. Bye. Bye. I love you. Bye. Cheery grins from ear to ear. Soon, several weeks had run out. Chagrin from here to here. I just called, to say, I love yoooooou. Oh, that's so sweet. I was just thinking how very much in love with you I am. Oh, you *are* a sweetie. It's because I love you. Yes, yes you *do,* don't you? Say it, I *need* it, *tell* me. Okay, I love you.

It didn't really work this time; it didn't really work the next, after that, it stopped working altogether.

6: Really Really Really Living

Star spangled, but never enough, it seemed one could not overdose smoking weed; we tried, well, *I* did, but found it a self-governing sedative, 'whiteys' preventing any harm that could be claimed as the main cause of death. Well, this was no good at all. Instead of going out in a blaze of glory as promised by 'drugs', we'd been kippered, up on tenter-hooks, a glaze of borey input.

Pass the lighter. Here, catch. Woah, did you see that? What? That. *What? That.* No. *This.* Oh, woah. Yeah, have a go. Hoho, to you. Haha, to you. Hoho, to you. Haha, to you. Hoho, to you. Tedium alleviated. Catch; simple catch, but with the back of the hand, with the onus on the thrower to make a catchable catch, made as awkward as possible with tricky-spin'n'perilous-arcing towards fragile or sharp obstacles, table edges, face-shots, surprise substituted 'balls' and all. Fun fun fun. We set about spilling the ashtrays into thick shag carpet by leaping clumsily around the easily upturnable coffee-table 'net', laughing hard.

Our front door always open to visitors, we were rarely alone, the beating heart, throbbing-liver'n'blackened-lung of a thriving creative community, a smoking-room where philologers'n'artists could meet over cups of sweet milky tea to discuss how to get involved in fun events: bands, orchestras, high-theatre, theatre, low-theatre, musical-theatre. Without needing to leave the room, nor rise from the settee, an ever-expanding range of strange unpaid *'opportunities'* were offered kindly for *'free exposure'.* Yes, yes yes yes yes, I'm your man, I'll be there, you can count on me, *I'm* a responsible adult. Playing partners exponentiated without qualitative scrutiny as determination resolved to make the most of *every* opportunity. Large slabs of time dedicated'n'promised, every other weekend taken; obelisks to squeeze a life around.

As the days rolled by, new arrivals pumped life back into the student city. Through narrow slits in *our* venetian blind, at eye level for *my* settee, an abundance of conspicuous beautiful spirits tickled the belly and widened the eyes; the waking world became colourful, vibrant, vivid, a lively place to navigate, far superior to dreamscape's dark jerky suck; better than cyclical telly death and putrefying on a couch, girls'n'boys come out to play. Hooray.

While funerals rolled, we stumbled out, lolloping the few short yards to the local pub, glad the knees still worked, eager to reconnect with friends, keen to find out who'd made it back alive, *and* show the face about in vain optimism that a gorgeous hippy fresher would spring suddenly into the foreground; some hope with *these* teeth, but one can never know what might appeal to the eye of the odd sorts who *knowingly* date jazz-musicians.

I asked for a job from the near-spherical landlord, sat in his usual spot by the door, perched on three particularly solid stools. He wheezed something in Ecky-thump that needed translation into Southern. On the third or fourth attempt, it transpired that he'd said something about needing help on weekend evenings. *Orl weekends, or neya fettle.* Ah, sorry, no, weekends are show-time; music *must* take priority, *that's* why I'm here, otherwise I'd be somewhere else doing other things, have you got any weekday shifts for a committed weekend musician? I implored lightly. Nur, he rasped, spluttered, coughed'n'croaked heftily.

We drank. I loved drinking. Drinking turned off the world. Something inside went ahahahahaha. Ahahahahaha, it went. Ahahahahaha.

What's so funny? Dunnow, this's grey', *yoo'r* grey', *thay*'grey', 'ello yooo, loo'queue, *yooor* grrrrrey', lie'queue'lots, wasssaaaaah.

Sifting crowds, overloaded somewhat, stuck in a rutting mode, a battle raged to keep the animal from poking through the shorts; tucked up in the elastic waistband, under a big'n'baggy tee-shirt, a jumper tied tightly around the lot to strap it in place properly.

Small talk became a big thing, big talk vanished under the instruction of: The Hippy Way; live'n'let live, dude, don't stare, don't *dare* point at people's differences, promote animal welfare, and don't smother, mother, or invade any other, man, yeah.

Hark unto the drinkless hippy who runs barefoot into the glass-strewn bar proclaiming that: no one should be allowed to say such phrases as: God is Dead, in case a stranger who *can't* defend their views, or *might* be frightened to, or *cannot* walk away from insult, or walk *around, might* take offence, *maybe*. Nature'n'nurture; Nietzsche'n'Nuremberg; nursemaids'n'nappies. The God debate arrived, but only to question if He could be a She. God exists. Proovit. God doesn't exist. Proovit. God's a girl. Ah, shuddup. I took offence, and sat on it, away from the others.

Thankfully, the pub had installed a video-jukebox over the summer, glitzy cleavages twinkled across the room in full-colour guilt-free panavision. I'd find a table with a clear view in the early afternoon, and sustain a rock-hard erection until closing.

On time, rag-week caused its usual rumpus up at the banner-strewn university campus. Free condoms everywhere, sexual success expected, even by the authorities; we filled a large bowl.

Couples sprung once more from nowhere. Cool chaps arrived with super-model beaus at their elbows; good-looking girls with slime; it was time to climb onboard the locomotion before the remaining lovelies got snaffled up, but the train doesn't stop for sluggish foot-shufflers who can't allow themselves to be seen staring at breasts'n'bums, when that is the first clue looked for.

Oh, so, you're with *him* now, but but but wasn't *he* with *her*, and *her*, and *her*, and *her*? The short-list of perfect 'possibles' depleted as news of relaxed sexual proclivity spread; at once, a delight *and* haunting horror to know objects of desire had shared their love amongst known infected 'friends' whose ghostly faces now leered over shoulders. Soon it seemed that none were free from the knowing looks of smug groin-scratching bed-notchers.

UNIVERSITY OF LOVE pt.2

7: Marks

College started with the news that there'd be gigs in the bar, hooray, and that they'd managed to lose all the world-class young-blood professors over a paltry pay dispute, booooo. General teaching standards dropped dramatically in the same year that freshers newly had to pay their teaching fees, poor buggers. The air of malcontent out-stunk the steaming students.

Only one class-lesson fitted with a personal learning curve: Mondays, 9 a.m., Advanced Harmony. For the second year running, Monday dawn starts and weekend excesses collided head-long. Jolt awakenings to class-mates laughing and teacher tutting were the year's most memorable lessons learned by a fair distance.

The bass teacher had gone in the walk-out, not *such* a bad thing for me; my end-of-year performance exam marks hadn't been encouraging, pinned to the notice board for anyone to gawk'n'giggle at; a knife through the eye, impaling-stick inserted.

An exact *bare* pass, exactly; not one single mark more, nor less, or fewer, or whatever; a message of some kind, one imagines. It didn't go unnoticed that the very *best* exam result for double-bass *and* bass-guitar, marked by one tutor, who'd walked out, presumably angrily, was several percentage points lower than the *worst* piano-exam mark, graded by a contended old-timer.

New academic year, new teachers, fresh exam, nothing to lose. I decided to play the same solo pieces as before, in the exact same manner, with the same few go-to tricks, as similarly as bare-pass talent allowed recreation of. We weren't supposed to pull such sneaky wool-caps, but there would be no ethical conundrums for the new tutors, they didn't know, or have a care, whereas I, on the other hand, could use the opportunity to find out if it were possible to adjudge jazz-judges objectively, or not.

It seemed a fair test, so I gave it my best; identical as possible, except, of course, that the examiners were different. Of two given marks, one of which was too high to be allowed, my lowest mark, pinned to the notice board to wow'n'wonder at, was: a first.

An exact *bare* first, exactly; not one single mark more, or less, or fewer, or whatever; a message of some kind, one imagines.

Sadly, for 'music academia', such disparate marks confirmed that the high-art of jazz and, possibly, music more generally, *cannot* be judged objectively. Although any could've guessed at that, it came as news to me; confirmed news, for either I'd improved *without* tutorage, or I'd been purposefully poohed previously.

In jazz exams, if the widest variable affecting one's mark is: how examiners *feel*, then what could be the value of an exam marked in this way? Some might've said, it *couldn't* be valuable. Annoyingly, this would never have been a problem, were I not enrolled on a jazz-course, majoring in performance. Three-years awaiting results of a coin-flip. One down. Tick. Two to go. Tock.

In some ways, with a happy result tucked into my cap, I felt lucky to have been given a chance to raise my game through the encouragement of not being down-graded for personal reasons; an opportunity to freshly flatter'n'fawn for healthier grades, but, in other ways, now 'knowing' that jazz performance exams were worse odds than a craps shoot, *that* bubble had well'n'truly burst. Pop.

The Student Union Office at the College was a pokey, informal affair. I turned up to get a SU card at the very first opportunity so to escape the clutches of the costly, cold, empty, vibeless caff-bar, so to go'n'hang out in the warm, full, groovy bars at the Uni. No one was ever about, so, to get the cards ordered, I became College SU President as a kind of joke, but then got lumbered with it permanently. We held weekly meetings until people stopped coming; when people stopped coming, I stopped going; when I stopped going, I dunnow what happened, I wasn't there.

8: Proper Conduct

My love life thus far didn't count, as described, all aspects of it negated themselves out, by unsound reckoning I *assumed* that I'd be due a proper shot at togetherness somewhere along the line. Long distance relationships were no longer an advertised part of the local agenda; I wished once again, as so many of us do, to fall in lust with a nearby nympho, that would be excellent. I made it known, to any who'd listen, that I was a randy tiger on the prowl, eager to orgasm in company; a martyr to polite chastity no more.

Looking to attract a musical partner, I continued saying yes, yes yes yes yes to more'n'more musical things, getting out there out *there*, where talent circulated *outside* the music college.

Purely for reasons of interest, the music college jazz course contained mostly blokes, that's jazz. Up at the university, however, music events were awash with girls. Obligation done'n'dusted, I'd climb the tall hill in pursuit of higher-frequency interaction with emotionally intelligent sorts, hoping to run into favourite feminine folk by happy accident. Sitting about university campus displaying my ignorance, so that passionate eyes would take time to school me, brought significantly more joy to the ailing heart than any simmering sizzleless sausage extravaganza ever would.

Over-excited, I'd agreed to conduct the University Wind Band, taking over the weekly role from my pilot who'd moved up the conducting ranks; patently unfit for the task as a stringy double-bassist, I still turned out to be one of the best qualified within poking distance, given any arbitrarily short pole-length. After a first nervous rehearsal, I found out that the wind band secretary fancied me. Yay. My pilot dropped big winky hints, sniggering at some peculiar piece of information available only to himself; telling me to *wink* *prepare for anything* *wink*.

Accepting her invite to dinner, partly on the premise that we had repertoire decisions to make, partially on a speculative date, I smartened up, scrubbed up'n'down, then nervously mooched the hundred yards to her place in my cleanest shorts. At the corner shop, I emptied the pockets for a cheap bunch of old flowers, cheap wine, and enough beer for courage. Knock knock.

She poured herself better wine and cooked vegetarian food like a real grown-up while we chatted on stools in the kitchen. We discussed alcohol, politics, religion, *sex*; we confused swing-music for couple-swapping, oh, *how* we laughed. Sex, ahahaha.

At the very next moment, her previously unmentioned bi-sexual boyfriend arrived home not entirely displeased to see me. *Hello honey,* I'm home. Hello love. Darling. Oh. Oh? Oh, um, hell, er, hello, *whow* are you? I'm the boyf, and I'm *fine* thank you, nice shorts, oh, and, er, flowers, how, um, lovely. We've been *working.* Ohahahokay then, anything fun? Wind band. Oh, it's *you,* she's told me all about *you,* well, I'm gonna take a bath if anyone wants to join me? Okay, hah. *Yeah, great,* will we all fit in do you think? Oh! Oh? Oh, no, thanks though. *No?* Yes. *Yes?* No. *No?* Yes, no. Yes *and* no? No, *no*'n'*no.* So, no. Yes, *no.* Yes? No. Not yes? Er, n*yeees?* Yes you would, or no you would? No I woah, hey, stop it. Oh, penises a problem are they diddums; haven't *you* got one?

Are you alright? *Uh?* Are you alright? *What?* You just phased out there. *Oh,* I'm fine thanks. Are you sure? Ahahahahaha, yeah, where'd he go? He's running a bath, did you want to jump in?

Cerberus raised its heads. Slaying this beast would give the anti-priest dominion over Hell's gate. Time to exorcise a demon.

Do it. Let's do it. I'm gonna do it. We're gonna really do it.

Oh, no we're *not! Wah! Nnnnnngh,* nonononono, not yet ready for a naked man sat fiddling on the staircase. Trigger boom bang. Drinking stopped; talking stopped; all interaction stopped. Click. But your wine, beer, the nut roast, we've not chosen a program. Slam. Home, shell, bed, arse kicking.

9: Improper Conduct

A different *single* girl from the wind band showed an interest. Conductors'n'electricity, I started working on a joke. Nervous, wide lovely eyes, well-spoken, a companion with whom to share affairs of the heart *fairly* openly. Pigeon steps. Pidgin truths.

Late at night, she'd invite herself in for a snog'n'cuddle on the couch, weirdly ostracising my pilot'n'guests, were they about. The polite thing to do would've been to whisk her away to the bedroom, but no, she refused gentle coaxing, yet kept whispering quietly in my ear. Embarrassment broiled'n'blushed; none of *his* girlfriends ever behaved so rudely; so *very* uncool. Eventually, she begrudgingly yielded to some frank advice, from another girl.

Over several weeks, nightly, we'd lie together under thumping holding hands tightly, talking of world affairs, love'n'philosophy. She shared some deep secrets, I shared some shallow secrets; she wanted one partner, we *both* did; she didn't like to be naked, nor me; she wanted to go slow, I wanted to chivvy things along, or, for her to stop disturbing my alone time with conversation when I could've been masturbating, or *we* could've. Bedroom rules were laid down: an orgasm each, preferably many *many* more.

One night, she turned up drunk. So, get the condoms, this is happening. *Condoms?* Condoms. But. Condoms. But. Condoms. Butwhydon'twejustplayabitandhavesomefun? Condoms.

The communal stash had all gone. The all-night shop had shut. She slept soundly upon my return. The next day, I stocked up, three should do it. She returned a few nights later to try again, however, the fiddle'n'discomfort pinching'n'pinging caused three rather urgent trips to squat awkwardly over the cold tap. Happily, we ran out before any serious damage could be done, as we started to get a feel for smiling'n'spooning *semi*-naked.

The following week, desperate offers of touchy-feely foreplay refused, we'd managed to get a more expensive condom to stay on, just about, again the last one in the pack, so she climbed on top taking a giant-leap of kindness for this man. A metaphorical wedding ring pushed its way over an allegorical shrink-wrapped cucumber. Shortly, done with the agony of it, we took turns in the bathroom to nurse our burns'n'abrasions. The condom itself had split from base to tip, but, as contraceptive, it'd worked perfectly.

In the morning, and onwards, our easy relationship changed. She turned hard of face, losing her coy delicacies; no longer popping by for late-night housemate-snubbing snogs. Her phone rang off the hook, but, without her address, I could only wait up hoping for a late night knock, each'n'every night staring blankly at static, dead behind the eyes, failing to comprehend the bleak enormity of maintaining *two* bone-dry relationships, at this, or at any other time of life, but mostly at *this* time of life. That's it, you've had your wicked way, that's your fill until divorce, a lifetime's worth; ownership has been settled for wheeling out at dinner-parties'n'family-gatherings, *they* know what *you* did.

Gutted was I by this change of focus, and cold, empty settee. Lonely nights thumped away, head in a distant vat, sponging up tomorrow's many events; mulling mentally structured logistics; preparing the body for the vigorous athletic undertakings ahead. Slumber rarer than blue; zzzzz, dream, floating faces, aaaaargh, click, breathe, up'n'out to reawaken slowly under the double basting, bee-sting eyes cracking to familiar bumpy paving on the toilsome trek into town, to slap the plank with musical strangers.

Paying karmic debts were of the highest priority at this time, living up to and *exceeding* the expectations of others, *all* others, everyone altogether. By pleasing *most* people, *most* of the time, I'd rebalance the energy for being a right bastard to a mere few. And so, the hierarchy of needs reformed, starting with double-bass needs. Lady Music, the *only* reason to be raising debtors.

There may not have been much integrity flying around, but working up to maximal integrity seemed to be the done thing; turning up early, ready to start on time, pulling the same way in the same place at the same time, each playing our chosen rôle. Whoever we were, wherever we were, *we'll* turn up to perform; side by side, hand in hand, we're a band together, bomb bomb.

Diary, a mess of music, fit-to-burst with rehearsals'n'gigs, switching playing venues at speed, only to annoy two sets of musicians by arriving late, or leaving before *notes,* or drinks. Time pressures also distressed the phone-message girl-friend of adulterous possibility by not being around for impulsive capers when called upon at a moment's notice, *or* arriving late'n'sweaty.

Conducting the wind band filled me with pride; people turned up keenly expecting *me* to pull things into shape. Whip, whip, hooray. Plus, girls, obviously. Though the plan had vaguely been to find *the* girl, not just *girls,* nor just *any* girl, and especially not just *a* girl who actively tormented choices made to act in the best interest of the maximum number of people, most of the time, mostly. Before wind band would start, open diary in hand, she'd demand public affection; *demand*, to my face, without smiling, *and* demand that I cancel booked musical activities to see her. Funny, I hadn't initially put her down as completely bloody mad. She could have every spare minute, but she didn't want *that then*, which *could* be done, oh no, she wanted *that then*. Hooked on her snagged line; transfixed by her severe nature; joyful she cared enough to be furious, I'd be left blinking in awe'n'bafflement at the scolding derision poured on my decisive hierarchy of needs; she'd twist the knife and I *deserved* it, nevertheless, hopeful of affection, I'd flirt, but not obviously, as per her strict instruction.

Tit for tat, stroppy, proud'n'belligerent, the both of us doubly doubled down; for my part, agreeing to ever more musical activity, *my* schedule *my* own, to make unbearable as *I* see fit. Nur.

Weeks curdled. Love's poverty in daily life delved the very values of survival, for there could be no unpaid rehearsal more important than spending the actual time of one's actual life with an actual partner; nothing more critical than declaring spiritual bonds publicly by *being there*, which was the main reason for our fling in the first place, as she'd keep reminding me in our few weekly minutes together, where cuddling would be cheered so messages of wanton lust were disguised professionally, until kisses'n'flirting in the dark'n'sweaty bar afterwards, as is the traditional time'n'place for scaredy-cats to display such things.

Fryday-night-drinks, jazz-hands, *the* fully budgeted booze-up; I'd starve myself in preparation. Wind band folk all hanging out while I, their intrepid leader, would be moping about like a disowned lamb, evertheless hopeful of affection, ever in trouble for having missed some house-party, or luncheon, or double-date, or other social event that she'd planned to show me off at, at an hour's notice. Just for the record, some rehearsals *were* more important than lazing in the park, when that was the offer.

One such evening, when she'd headed to the bar particularly bothered about some *thing* or other; some significant periphery; some passion neglected; some perceived slight hidden and left unnamed; some unknown friend accidentally insulted by my not having ever met them, having not been somewhere, due to being somewhere else, or *some* shit; from *nowhere*, I declared a sudden heated desire for her easy-going best friend, *to* her best friend.

Cheese'a'nappy, soam'aye, jazz'canon'may'crap'*ick,* can't'nt, no'*ev'nev'ev'may'crappy,* i's'snop'possble, i'snot, i's's'*imp'possble*, east'oo'ard, cheese'jazz'n'nappy'in'ear: a'mean'ewe, loo'cashew, luke'achoo, jazz'loo'queue, yoo'jazz'grey'ooze', yoo'soap'er'f'*ick*, n'yoo'n'mee'n'yoo n'mee'n'yoo'n'me'd'bee'jazz'purr'feta'getter; butt'meat'achin'; g'nutella, mm'gonad'oo'*ick,* mm'g'nag'ovum, mm'gnu'gove'umm, mm'go'ova'errr, goat'swerver'cheese'scone, n'm'mm'g'nutella'wee'rover, cosh'mean'snuff'*ick,* nuffinktoomy.

Nuffinktoomy?   Oh, y'ba'*ick*, *grey*, ummm, errr, niarrhoea agot't't'say'sump'th'*ick*, a'got't't'ell'yoo, 'yoo'yoo'bootfull'yoo, a'v'av'v'may'dave'err'dissifult'denishon, deshizzun, de'cis'shun, cor'swell'troo'th'*ick* weir'snot'grate, wee'snow'goo', yawn'nappy, anne'diamond'nappy'swell, ant'simarlily, *similarl'ick, cozz'zz'zs*, wee'snot'gooty'get'th'*ick*, snot'got'I'm'av'wee? ...gutter'cossetrate on'emu's's'*ick*, 'swy'm'ere. *What do you mean:* **nothing to you?**

The two of them refused to engage in further monversation, squinting, whispering, wandering away, herself first, her friend left behind with the memorable message: *she* thinks that *you* are scum, which was totally fair in this instance, and more widely.

She stopped coming to wind band and vanished into the ether. I stopped drinking, for a bit. Time juddered along contemplating if The Dales could supply a picturesque enough peak to inspire a fitting finish, or if this coward even had the bus-fare back.

I worried for her, and for my precious reputation, which had become an unwanted thing, having toyed briefly with the idea of a life prolonged. Sober heartbeats clanged loud'n'thumply as the reverb of her shadow drowned out everything bar the tubas. Fear of a rape-claim loomed'n'looped around a mind expecting and well-prepared for the 'very' worst. Rational, or, irrational? The box containing *that* box was sealed; unopened, unopenable.

Her best friend, who *didn't* hate me, but, in solidarity, had stayed away, returned to the merry depleted fold, so, on bended knee, I begged *her* to pass a message on to *herself* to come back.

One day, they snuck in together after down-beat. Eyes resisted connection; current charges ground away as I diode inside, shocked, anode, rehearsing only watt hertz most; hertz schmerz.

I'm not sure exactly what I thought the blubbing was about, running out of that fateful rehearsal in a gush of public tears, emotion freely flowing as the three of us sat down to talk it through slowly'n'sensibly, clearing the air like proper grown-ups, and a snivelling snotty kid. I apologised, and they were kind.

10: Gig Economy

Gig economy? Hah! If only. Before gigs happen, there's the *rehearsal* economy; paid in smiles, cups of tea and, often, booze; too often, and yet, one *might* say, not often enough; *I* might say. Not being one to shy from the next round, personal debts mounted, to be paid off when fully qualified as, um, as a jazz musician.

Rehearsing on busy days, as the last note faded away, double-quick, bass packed, off to the next rehearsal with the next band starting *now*. Next week? Midweek? Sunday? Morning? Really? *Really?* Everyone? Okay, it's in the diary, see'ya'then'gotta'go, bye. Slip away swiftly before the drummer realises they've a gig, or garden party, or whatever damn thing booked in on Sunday. Gotta keep going: getting out, staying out, staying up, getting up. Sunday arrives. Toddle toddle. Nnnnnngh. Toddle toddle.

Mercilessly steep hills traipsed, cold, wet'n'weary; life-force draining away with the full weight of cancellations and double bookings bearing down. Empathy? Fuck empathy. Some people just don't care a darntoot that one has been carrying a double hernia over several miles of hillock to arrive professionally early, *unnoticed,* squandering the precious vitality of invaluable youth to grind out a painful hour of pop with an ungiggable band of strangers, only to learn upon arrival that the pianist has decided they'd prefer to spend their precious winter morning warmly snuggled up to a loved one, or making children, or whatever.

Sat in the vibeless bar with placid bandleaders, I'd lose it. Well, *you* chose to play the thing. Yeah, *play* it, not lug it about only to sit next to it for no more than a cuppa as recompense, which, being the same price as a half of beer, I'll have instead, thanks very much, oh, what; you want to book another, really? Really. Well, er, um, erm, you'd better make it a pint then, cheers.

There is no rehearsal for life. Similarly, there's no need to rehearse if experimental experiential distraction is your thing. Experimental experiential distraction was definitely my thing.

I loved experimental experiential distraction. Experimental experiential distraction turned off the world. Something inside went woo-hoo-bloody-rah. Woo-hoo-bloody-rah, it went.

Woo-hoo-bloody-rah.

Experimental experiential distraction came around less often than hoped for, replaced by goals set by some mega-lo-maniac who'd want to achieve some *other* dead-end that needed more headspace than a simple: title, key, one two three woo-hoo.

Broadly, one shouldn't 'rehearse' 'jazz' much, by which I mean, of course, *improvised* jazz, the apex art-form of *any* civilisation, for that would set in stone a specific version of subtle events which can only be replicated imperfectly; whereas, if one doesn't rehearse, there is no unobtainable ideal that one could then fail to achieve, so, nothing can go 'wrong', if nothing can go 'right'.

By this reckoning, any rehearsal would be more beneficial being seat-of-the-teeth, skin-of-the-ears listening stuff, using the skills of those in the room instead of failing to replicate any given ideal in the mind of any given mega-lo-maniac on any given day.

By the act of rehearsing, we were propagating false ideals of karaoke stardom in overly-keen'n'underly-self-aware singers who believed they were going to break the world with *this* version of *this* cover-song with *this* set of musicians, tomorrow, by recreating some famous pre-recorded track they'd memorised note-for-note, with an unpaid band, without charts, or direction. Misguided sorts would call weekly rehearsals and then, far from exploring the further reaches of quantal interaction to push the social brain to create something amazing, musical development halted at first play-through into; two-to-a-bar, four-chord-cycle, root-fifth torture; no chromatic filler, round'n'round, over'n'over, and over, until vomit filled the mouth, or full mental prolapse.

Can you play it like last time, please? Er, I *can*, I *could*, I *would* *if* I wanted to, but no, I *shall* not; *will* not; for why'd anyone want to repeat the same thing over'n'over'n'over'n'over'n'over again? Well, it's helpful if we know what's coming, so, if you could play your solo the same each time, that'd be great. Um, you mean, the *improvised* solo, okay, no, I won't be doing that. But why not? Because I can already do that. Oh, well, oh. Er, yeah, quite, and if you want us to play rhythmic stabs invented on the fly, a month ago; if you want *anyone* to play the music *you* want to play in an arrangement *you* want played, write it on manuscript; oh, you don't read or write music, ah, okaaaaay, well, in that case, what you'll want to do is go and find yourself another double-bassist, and get yourself some theory lessons, or a loop pedal.

Mandatory bands, set up by the college to pass the course, were *most* dreaded. Ecstatic musical elations, found traversing new routes through harmonic patterns, were being worn thin by pointless repetition, permuting all available options in each direction without the reward of applause, or cash, or improved chance of procreation, echoing errors of the inversely talented as a pastime, chained to the college for a stream of very average saxophonists to squonk their way up'n'down blues-scales badly.

Except for a podgy baritone-saxophonist who'd *all* the skills, our *ensemble*, if that's the word, our *ragtag-band,* mangled the arrangements to within an inch of my life. Clearly, for some, the learning curve had plateaued early, such students, distributed by flip-a-coin marking methods now defined all 'academic' futures within earshot. Impatience nagged at smoke-deprived lungs as a fear of perceived hubris kept the loyal in their seats week after teeth-grinding week, going through motions; enduring absolute beginners for nothing, which is less than a full instructor's wage, or union rates, or a peripatetic fee, or amateur theatre 'envelope', or portage, or some, or one, or half, or negative one twelfth; epsilon nought deflated infinitesimally in the empty coughers.

Okay, is everybody, no, okay, fine, mouthpiece in? Alright? Everyone? Got the music? No? Mmmmmm, here, can you pass, great, from the top, a-one no, okay, alright, ready? And a-one, and a-two, and a-one two three four. Boop boop boppety bop boppety bop bop scooby dooby wooby doooby do wah do wop honk. Stop stop stop. Eff sharps, and again, from the top, a-one, and a-two, and a-one two three four. Boop boop boppety bop boppety bop bop scooby dooby wooby doooby do wah do wop honk. Stop stop stop. Eff sharp, fourth bar, third beat, and again, from the top, a-one two three four. Boop boop boppety bop boppety bop bop scooby dooby wooby doooby do wah do wop honk. Stop stop stop. Everyone play your concert eff sharps, no, it's.. no, that's a.. that's right, okay, bar four, keep your eyes open, and again, and a-one two three four. Boop boop boppety bop boppety bop bop scooby dooby wooby doooby do wah do wop honk. Stop stop stop. Effing eff effing sharps *please* people, just run the fourth bar, and again, *good,* now, from the top, *slowly.*

Stop stop stop, I'm off, this is just awful. Oh, don't pack away. No fear, I'm not helping by being here, what *you* want is some one-on-one time with your horn section. But, we are *all* here to improve, do you really think that leaving us without a double-bass player is gonna help us *all* improve? Honestly, it would be fairly hard to prevent it. Well, do you think *you'll* improve by walking away? Getting better already by mean-average, I reckon. Do you think that *I want* to give *my* time for *you* to walk away? For money, um, yeah, I do, *I* would, look, it's not you, it's me, and *them*, I don't care, I want out, right now, sorry, but I cannot bear and *will not* suffer it; marks don't matter, a jazz degree really *really* doesn't matter, *nothing* matters except that this godawful noise is distanced by walls from these overly-sensitive ears. Don't you *want* to play my recently dead cousin's arrangements? Yes, er, no, um, *quite,* life is a-wasting, I've got to *earn enough to* smoke, immediately; I'm off to busk on my own, bye. But. Bye.

11: Engels

That a musician might enjoy living the life of a musician, potentially, is one of the many accusations leveled at musicians by non-musicians. Well, at least you enjoy it mate. Nnnnnngh.

Youthful impetus gone, drained; limping up with the double-barrel pump-action foot-spike to freebees in capitalist environs, pushed above'n'beyond for two forty-five's to no one. No cash, no marks for the degree, no bullet-point for the CV, no story for the book, no love, no fun, no joy. Pooh. In too deep to a life that *I'd* chosen but hated, worked into a tearful rage, I decided that *today* would be as good a day as any, and so hoisted the double-bass onto the shoulder for the last time, sniffed wistful goodbyes to no one important, wandered out of college and headed glumly toward loud traffic, when the podgy bari-player chased me down to suggest that we should be friends forever, go busking *together*, and that I should join his experimental trio with a guitar genius.

I immediately burst into tears, then kneeled down and kissed his chubby, thickly-haired fingers, like a real weirdo. Are you an Angel? Nine, itch benign doycher. What? I'm German. Aha, güt, ha, ich, er, um, oh, er, ich *did* jerdeutche, auf, er, der schule und, er, einen, um, ein D begotten. Ooookaaay, ja, ve'll spreak Anglish.

We'd both been looking for a skint musical busking partner prepared to put in the hours, combining two of the three main purposes of life into one time-saving hand-breaking activity. Unamplified, pain twang pain every pain note pain, poking the frozen claw into an ostrich-egg-slice for pennies; however, we had gumption, and were sufficiently good for the council reps to tell us as much, which was nice. As the year wound down, on any clear day, we'd chase folks up'n'down the streets to popular hits mangled flat until the winter chill curtailed our motor-facility.

As Christmas approached, the theatre groups got their shows squawking in the warm halls of the university, where one was never more than two-minutes from a subsidised drink, which I made *some* use of, although funds were limited, again, as ever, suicidal splurges had spent it all before beer'n'bills had been budgeted, but there were occasional pints for favours, as is not-quite-so-often-as-it-should-be the way in amateur arts.

Theataaah, daaahling. Treading the boards; staring at breasts without fear of being called a perve; girls stripped to the knickers running around in the wings picking at their bits. Awesome. Every evening, pitted in rhythmic root-fifth reverie, I'd day-dream of a lifetime spent getting old with the various talented creatives around, as I'd always done, and hoped others did too.

And so the weeks up to Christmas passed gawping lustfully; skint, sober, and drained of blood. Better strapping required. Nothing whatsoever could've restrained the mischievous animal. For good'n'ill, much time was spent hidden behind an enormous instrument designed to vibrate with a deep rumble that goes a long way towards erotic stimulation. In a very physical sense: love surrogacy, rubbing against something huggable'n'vibrating in the dark, had tricked the wandering mind into a form of active relationship bond with the uplit faces reflecting my fairly feeble flirtations favourably. See you at the after-show. Tee-hee.

Suddenly Saturdays became a problem. Bandleaders took last-minute seasonal do-or-die gigs for no money, at the moment when fully taken with the promise of after-show connection with creative types, any one of whom *could've* been *the* life-partner I'd've tried not to own, but would like to have come home to of an evening, or have come home to me, kind of a thing, if that's okay. Bands lay ultimatums. Saturdays *must* be for gigs; band *first,* before shit-fuck *musical-theatre!* Oh, uh, okay. The body double wife would take the brunt of my love'n'hate'n'love'n'hate'n'love, but mostly hate, as we'd trundle by the after-shows, just too late.

12: Higher Education

World as hamster-ball, rolling around inside a hollow sphere of seclusion, every footstep uphill. More. Bring it. Make it hurt. Rage, pain, anguish. Click. Jazzy jazz. Click. Fury, wrath, anger. Something inside went waaaaah. Waaaaah, it went.

Waaaaah.

Bored of walking bass, bored of lifting bass, bored of double-pack obstacle courses, bored of backache, bored of sore fingers; physically, metaphysically, all this burdenous baggage *had* to go.

At gigs, I'd noticed that comedians had *no* equipment, a mic., *maybe, and* no band to split the fee with, *and* most were rubbish, *I* could do that. *Sold,* to the kinked man with dropped shoulders.

Comedy. That's the new me. Yes, sirree. Pathos'n'slapstick and all that. Comedians are happy people, right? Well, okay, no, famously not, but levity would be as good a place to quest afresh as any, if walking about subjected to extra gravity wouldn't do it.

First things first, the laugh. Ahahaha-hur-hur-huh-huh-huh, done. Necessary although insufficient, the first step to humour; the opposite of crying tragically, but not giggable comedy just yet.

Next, original jokes, okay, God, You're up, I'll wait here. Tick.

Oh, hello, hey you two, before you dash off upstairs, I've been working on a joke; *ahem:* how do you know Jesu' had a broom? What are the jazz-hands for? Er, it's, um, this is the joke, it shows there's a joke coming, jazz-hands are my thing, I do jazz-hands now: so, how do you know Jesu' had a broom? I don't know what's wrong with you, are you having some kind of a seizure? *How'do'you'know'Jesu''had'a'broom?* Okay, *I'll* bite, *I* don't know, how *do* you know that Jesu' had a broom? *Ahem:* John 11v35, ahahaha-hur-hur-huh-huh-huh. It's not very good. *Goodnight! Nono,* it's *very* good. *Goodnight! Oh,* he didn't *mean* it. *Goodnight!*

It gradually dawned that comedians need something to say, plus brass balls to speak without falling to pieces on stage. Balls. I wouldn't last a second, filters all out of whack, taken down by the first heckle, staring into space, pondering ethical decisions slowly in front of the crowd'n'God. Oh, well, that's not going to work at all. Fine, I thought, as comedy wouldn't come naturally in the God-given flow required to make a sellable success of it, I'd have to pick it apart with gritty science, to find what *is* funny by removing that which is *definitely* unfunny, then whittle back what remains into puns that couldn't offend me, or my mum; *then* money'n'girls, *and* I'd be a lighter, more likeable, person.

So, what *isn't* funny? Oh, ah, oh. Silence, tubas, more silence.

Sex-crimes, depression, religion'n'jazz seemed an unlikely set of subjects to keep anyone's attention for even a short floor spot. Maybe the stage wouldn't be the best place to undergo therapy. Maybe thoughts such as mine *should* be hidden from public view. Maybe the entertainment industry wouldn't be right for me.

Realism brought intensely into focus by the big, red, shiny bills, time had run out on debts, income needed instantly. *Panic! Yes, all bad.* Dreams of therapy buried, desperate anxiety rocked empty mindscapes as the currency of known jazz-changes filled in where comedy wasn't. At least you enjoy it mate. Nnnnnngh!

Oh, hello, you're, um, back. Yeah, he's asleep and I wanted a ciggy, are you crying? No, just thinking; you know: putting the world to rights. Oh yeah, what're you thinking about? Actually, I'm trying to forget. Then what is it that you are trying to forget? Nnnnnngh, *great,* thanks for the reminder. *Tell* me. I'm trying not to. Open *up.* Let it go. It's *not* your *fault.* It *is.* Ha, it's *not* your fault. *Ugh,* it is a fault that starts'n'ends with *me,* so it's *my* problem. It may be your *problem* but it's *not* your *fault.* It's a fault in time'n'space that starts'n'ends'n'only exists 'cause of me, ergo. It's *not...* *Pleeeeease,* drop it; are you having fun up there? Oh, yeah, he's the *best;* okay, g'night. G'nigh. Tick. Tock. Bong.

Something nasty in the foreground. Bong.

Follow your dream they said. Follow your calling. Follow it off a cliff; into a tree; into gunfire. Trust'n'believe. Bong.

Something not quite forgotten. Bong.

Options, options, what are the options? Psychoanalysis? For *me? Really?* Am I particularly psychoanal? Maybe partly, maybe just the other part. Bong.

Something not quite remembered. Bong.

Maybe I could try philosophy or psychiatry as music-therapy wasn't working; I'd met a number of severely damaged people who'd ended up working as counsellors. Bong.

Something unseen obscured by background. Bong.

The space between: inside'n'outside, here'n'there, this'n'that, potentiality'n'possibility, opportunity'n'actuality. Bong.

Interactions yet to happen, never to happen, probability fields inverted upon the back of the eye. Bong.

Yawning chasms between dimensions, oceans unrecognised, as of yet'n'yet to be; arse of Yeti'n'Yeti beer. Bong.

Dynamic blankness inside cushions packed with nothingness unfilling the line between space'n'neighbouring spaces. Bong.

Nothing as an expanding thing in the world of thingly things that one has floating around in the tingly head. Bong.

Nothing, plus everything, minus something, the potential minds of Gods'n'men'n'women scrambled. Bong.

The unobservable universe, expanding into nothing. Bong.

Clouds of nothing sucked out of nowhere. Bong.

Nothing at all whatsoever, not expanding into nowhere. Bong.

Nothing itself, unexperienced as nothing, unfelt as nothing, unviewed as nothing, nothing with nothing not in it. Bong.

Nothing, left undescribed in its entirety. Bong.

Not even nothing. Zzzzzz.

Good morning comedian. Hmmhmmm, aaaaauuuuugh, good grief, fuck fuckety fuck, I'm late, *and* it's raining, bye. Hoist, slam.

13: Delusions

In mind's dark cavern, girthed broadly as a galleon, a double cardioid platform of finest brushed bronze, sparkling silver rails set in broken sections around its rim, tipping this way'n'that back'n'forth round'n'about atop a tapered plinth of solid stone; around the base, deep in the depths below, evil beings of limitless magical power brandish high-voltage king-cobra-poles, long vertical shafts no wider than a thumb, slapping at the sides, lighting up the railings above with a bright deathly crackle; hooded in Hessian robes, terrified monks cower in fear, clinging to the platform for their lives, lips'n'flaws fought over jealously; *soulswap;* nonononono, look down, clothed in over-sized habit, daemon's claws poke from sleeves, unable to find purchase, scrabbling helplessly on the frictionless surface, mustn't fall off, mustn't touch the rails, nonononono, slip under rails, swing out a limb instinctively to hang helplessly above a fall of certain death, crackle, nonononono, oh, survive injured with shielded talons, tip back the other way, sack body thrown in spirals across the rolling deck, sliding helplessly on clumsy rounded pincers, colliding with anything in the way, unwary monks sent spinning off haplessly into the void below with a shriek of horror, to be replaced a few seconds later with a more vicious pole slapping at the approaching railings, nonononono, zap; superheated bones roast the living flesh from the inside, zap; *soulswap;* nonononono, wooden stumps, fumble'n'tumble, zap; *soulswap;* nonononono, soapy tentacles, slip, slide'n'slither, zap; *soulswap;* nonononono, metal spikes, skate, skim'n'skid, zap; *soulswap;* nonononono, crunch; bits of skull, brains'n'inner organs ooze outside the skin as evil beings come in to feast on the living twitching flesh, slurp: *soulswap;* nononono... oh, let's get 'em, how does this pole work?

One bitter Winter morning, having just fallen off, I awoke with such a start that I kneed myself squarely in the face. One should listen to God when He speaks, so I took the day off, as instructed.

Sat downstairs, in the puddle-shaped hole near the window, self-pity skewered the useless shell to the sunken settee as the cheap digital phone erupted on the stairs for ten-minutes, or so, every hour, or so, hijacking calm with arhythmic chest thudding to sit blinking through daytime television in guilt'n'shame.

To this moment, I'd been as devoted as a dog in a tutu, but, now the worm had turgor, *I'd* become the arsepole ruining the strenuous efforts of others. I hated ruining the strenuous efforts of others. Ruining the strenuous efforts of others turned up the world. Something inside went nnnnngh. Nnnnnngh, it went. Nnnnnngh.

Despite negative aspects, it felt good not being ear-poked or finger-broked by every interaction, so I took the next day off too. This time, I phoned everyone, left messages, pulled the phone-cable out of the wall, turned electrical noises off, and silence.

Peace finally descended upon the house.

Aaaaaah.

Aaaaaah, aaaaah'n'aaaaah again, and aaaaah fuck it, also.

Waaaaah.

I'd no real desire to repair, much preferring the easy delirious decline into avoidance, but, with endless tea and thinking time, *something* was happening. As tired muscles inhaled, brain activity fired up, in gear. The return of the incredulous sulk. Think, orgasm, unthink, orgasm, maybe eat, maybe sleep, repeat. Paranoia paranoia paranoia paranoia paranoia pa............ ....aaaaaaaaaaaaaaaaaaaaaaaaaaaaaaah!

Stupidity rattled around in the widening cracks between expanding information sets; words as obstacles, insufficient to explain sad thoughts'n'feelings away; mush. Instead of wordly-wisdom disproving malism, Lady Music stepped in, looking fine.

Click. Malady. Click. M'Lady. Click. Melody. Click.

To improvise a melody had been my only aspiration in life, other than death, and love, and kharmic justice, since all that rotten mess. Changes played around in silence, again'n'again, and again; tight efficient learning, harmonic shapes morphing in loopy-loop space; fleeting extensions slowed'n'repeated until enough thread had been woven in to reveal complexities of flowing patterns pulsating through the fabric of each song. Tick.

And so it went each weekday morning, phoning bandleaders to half-heartedly apologise, hoping to leave messages just after they'd've needed to have left home, so that confrontation could be avoided, and then private practice without an instrument, working through The Real-Book beyond the 'A' section without plucking blisters or grating human-malaise to prevent absorption.

I could hear God speaking to me, and He spake thusly: Distractions Are Too Distracting. And there it stands: the most inane observation ever made, still, I aspired to my God's word. Nur.

After weeks of hiding out, missing lectures to avoid meeting rehearsal obligation'n'stress, inspired by clarity of mind that'd appeared after big, broad, brush-stroke decisions, I phoned all college bandmates, and quit, for good, forever, for now. Bye. But. Bye. But. Bye. But. Bye. But. Bye. But. Bye. But. Bye-bye.

Freedom. Glorious freedom.

All gone, except for wind band, and *one* originals three-piece who played fun music to groove to, which is the point of music for non-musicians, who've got the money to buy the tickets to see live music. Plus, the most stunning woman I'd ever stood within twenty-feet of would come to our gigs, look at me, smile, and talk to me after we'd played as if I were somebody worth knowing, which went a long way towards deciding which of sixteen bands could be allowed to continue weaving tapestries across the inside of the creased, cramped'n'cluttered forehead.

And relax.

We're informed by certain misanthrops that: the *illegal act* of smoking marijuana *causes* paranoia. The next claim to this end, more an observation, is that: a smoker cannot refute the claim, nor broach the subject, without seeming a tiny bit paranoid.

Dare it be said in reply, before knowing if the bio-chemistry plays out, that: tying oneself in knots to refute accusations of paranoia, is in itself an irrefutable cause of *symptoms* of paranoia.

The dictionary states clearly'n'concisely that: *Paranoia* is; *mental derangement with delusions of grandeur, or persecution, etc.; an abnormal tendency to suspect and mistrust others.*

Abnormal seems to be the operative word in this description, it implies that somebody somewhere knows just what it is that a *normal* tendency to *suspect'n'mistrust others* should be.

A *normal* civilian might say that: an *illegal act* is *an illegal act,* whatever the *illegal* activity; whichever the law system; Holy, Common, or foreign, don't do *illegal* stuff, it's *illegal.* If a *fairly normal* person then performs *an illegal act*, it *must* invoke *symptoms* of paranoia; *grandiosely* placing oneself above a law that *is* policed by *actual* police with truncheons will do that. *Suspicion'n'mistrust* of others with, let us say, information concerning *an illegal act*, so that loose tongues don't blab to the wrong people, is a behaviour learned in infancy to avoid trouble; guarded word choice comes from a genuine position that 'they' *can* come and 'take you away' at any moment for *an illegal act.*

It *could* be said that, if it *were* legal; distributed'n'sold from post offices, then the problem of village post offices closing down in the Nineties would've been solved in that reality. In another reality, regulation would mean: choice, as with all legal things, no getting ripped off by criminals, or arrested; thousands of brilliant botanists would be freed from prison to rejoin the economy, hundreds of thousands of self-medicators would be free to self-medicate, and tens of millions of hours would be given back to the police to fight crime, which there'd be less of. Aaaaaanyway.

Criminals forcing injustice upon others, in a system that allows them to get away with it, causes *symptoms* of paranoia. Victims of trauma may feel the need to medicate with sedatives to calm feelings of raging injustice that spring from empirically verifiable examples of invasive *persecution;* a medical condition. So, so as to be socially sensitive, before knowing an individual pot-smoker's back-story, blanket 'diagnoses' of *paranoia* would be best avoided, even if circumstantial primary evidence backs up the claim, one should not try to crush the partially crumpled.

Maybe an over-sensitivity to being labeled *mentally deranged,* at a time of peak emotional instability, will instil a sense of determined underachievement in the mind of the unrepentant smoker, to under-play successes as proof that 'the accusers' are wrong about smoking being the *cause* for *symptoms* of paranoia. Known *symptoms* of such reflexive reflective psychoses include: *not grandiosely speaking well* of one's proficiencies'n'prospects, and *hiding perceptions of persecution* when therapy is required.

When *mental derangement* is, in one form or another, known by the user as first cause'n'reason to self-tranquillise in hope of inner quietude, any *suggestion* of: a *threat* of: *impending mental derangement,* will be seen for the unlapped claptrap that it is. That the herb in question, 'used' for having subdued the wildest of sober *derangement* effectively'n'repeatedly, is claimed to be a root *cause* of the *symptoms of paranoia* that needed quelling *before* the first dose had been taken, sorry, but no, that's not a fair test, neither madness nor chronology work like that. If a trauma victim finds an inner tranquility smoking, then gets to the quack to be diagnosed as suffering from paranoid *symptoms,* figures skew *against* the palliative; have skewed. It's cruelty to suggest that alleviation of suffering is the wrong course of action. Don't take *those* effective drugs: take *these* random drugs that have the seal of approval from the government and the taxable drugs companies, but first, admit you're mad'n'suicidal. Drugs. Yeah.

Financial obligation instills *symptoms* of paranoia in those with unbalanced books: students, jazz musicians, actors, poets, and the like, but again, it's not *derangement* to feel crushed by the weight of the world; to the contrary, digging oneself deeper into debt, as a pastime, really *does* cause *symptoms* of paranoia.

When trapped by debt-piles mounting around'n'about, with no obvious source of income, or timeline to earn; when food money as yet unearned is owed, and there is no credit available for repayment, metered-time passing sits heavy on a living heart; when computers say 'no' to a student, jazzer, poet, creative, etc., humans *will* exhibit *symptoms* of paranoia, because one's potential *has* been valued as worthless, or valueless, or hopeless, or whatever. Sweating long shifts, panicking that one's life is to be pulled from under one's feet, or sitting still, trying not to panic about the fact that one's life is to be pulled from under one's feet, or losing faith *because* one's life *has* been pulled from under one's feet by one's own error, *or* other folks errors, to a greater or lesser degree; *any* such states of impasse cause *symptoms* of paranoia. For it is well-known, when a summons states that: Enforcement Agents are to be set upon one's personage, *persecution* correctly describes *symptoms* one is *meant* to feel; provoked into anxiety by carefully crafted bubbling doubling costs every few weeks; a genuine threat to life'n'limb, and libido, as bailiffs *do* break *actual* bones, *do* kick balls, *do* accidentally kill people, and *do* steal stuff, for failure to fulfil payments on time.

The *symptoms* of paranoia, but *not* itself paranoia, these feelings are *not abnormal*, *not delusional*, they are *real* feelings caused by *real* threats of violence. However well a threat can be hidden by softspeak, a threat is still a threat, of, maybe, violence, and if there is nothing one can do about one's financial situation, as student, or creative, or whatever, then a threat of violence is just that: a threat, of violence, backed by Judges'n'Government, Chancellor'n'Treasury blessed, hanging over each'n'every knock.

Putting all one's faith in one's own ability to perform to a level to make a commercial success of it causes *symptoms* of paranoia. Any sensible citizen should know it is a *grandiose* statement of intent *indeed* to have enough self-belief to not drop everything creative for the first menial service job that comes along to pay the bills that otherwise mightn't get paid, possibly *ever*. And yet, conversely, to drop a fully laden egg-basket whilst in the throws of youth is the biggest *derangement* of all, ask any decent hippy. Don't give up on your dream, dude, unless your dream is ownership of other humans, or war, or being a total dick, man.

Unpaid bills; unpaid days; the magical love of a good tune being sucked from the room, watching others soar'n'squonk, rooted to one at each bar, not even one; making hard decisions; living unobserved; wanting to be elsewhere, wishing to snuggle, hoping to see a loved one; impending phone-calls, deadlines; replacing the milk'n'sugar, answering a door two-feet away, crying until vomit, determining to do a thing, and then doing it, fitting in with society, or not, it's all the same experience when outgoings exceed incomings, feelings *symptomatic* of paranoia.

Giving up loyalty to a younger-self's clear-cut b.&w. thinking; itching to *share* tough decisions that have taken years to decide; living with choices that can't be cited, to family extra-especially; being closed off from conversation causes *symptoms* of paranoia.

Lies cause *symptoms* of paranoia. Lying to oneself and others, giving-up lies, living a lie-free life, going from one state to the other; owning up; therapy; tackling untold horrors as balance oneself a hero'n'victim to different segments of society; 'loving' lies, hidden truths, differing degrees of different lies to different people, and, of course, finding out you yourself have been lied to causes *symptoms* of paranoia, schizophrenia, and other mental illness too; as neural pathways reify along their easiest course, synapses splitsplatsplot raw anxiety into on-off parts of the brain to be dredged up when *not* feeling oneself, if ever that may happen.

Psychotherapists won't go near the subject with a barge-pole, but theological lies *cannot* be denied, they hold special privilege in society as margarine untruths that are allowed to be spread and they *cannot* be denied; they spring forth from the mouths of our nearest'n'dearest and they *cannot* be denied; they have laws protecting their right to be spread and they *cannot* be denied; they splurge forth from our own sputtering mouths and they are almost always denied, though one *may* think that they *cannot* be.

Faith is inherently a *delusion of grandeur;* to convince oneself of any axiom of personal belief without sufficient proof, because *He* says so, ohoho, maybe not, but they'n'they and they say so; *sometimes* even *I* say so. *Persecuted* mindsets are forged in The Fire of Ridicule after sharing faith in front of closed doors while expecting everyone to care. Separatism by faith really does limit conversation to flash-tapping between the calcium carbonate ovoids, to avoid vacuously voicing divisive visions of The Void.

A religious truth, or religious lie, or whatever, *has to be* a *derangement* of the mind, which, coupled with any *delusion* one cares to share, goes some way to explain why every religious person since faith began has felt that others are teasing them. Nur.

Delusions of grandeur. One true religion. Tick.
Mistrust and suspicion of others. No other true religions. Tick.
Delusions of persecution. They ain't delusions. Tick.
Mental derangement. Faith ain't fact. Tick.

Preachers cause *symptoms* of paranoia. There cannot be an *abnormal: suspicious mistrust* of soothsayers, people have proven themselves unreliable as deliverers of 'The Truth' time'n'time and time again. It is *normal* to think that people are usually out to lie, in *some* form, when in all noticeably important cases, empirically, as *I* do, *they* have done, and *they* do, and *they* will do, so long as people exist to insist on *their* version of events with a Holy Book clutched in one hand and a tambourine in the other.

Close people, *trusted* people, friends'n'family being lied to; *spreading* a lie, passing it off as 'True', passing it on as 'True'; evangelising missionaries positioning themselves strategically around the world to spread evermore fervent lies to the furthest reaches of the planet; warped untruths, given freely with love; alternative reality burgeoning, lies upon lies sharing one parasol.

Renouncing a Holy Book, due to the enormous weight of such a thing, puts oneself *grandiosely* above one's family and their whole cultural world, *persecuted* by Satan's demons'n'devils; Hell-Hounded by earnest prayer'n'appeals to know'n'love Jesus, or whoever, as *they* know'n'love Jesus, or whoever, or Whoever, or whatever. Having been through the long prologue of doubting Holy Writ, bit by bit, it had been found less useful for learning than any other information pertaining to anything; theology stinks bad. *God,* though, eh? Lord Creator of all the *ologies.*

Giving up God? Unthinkable. My God'n'I were just about on speaking terms. Now'n'again I'd stare at the ceiling and roll my eyes as if to say: thanks for nothing, in as humourous way as I dare, right up to the edge before it could've been reclassified as: a blasphemous sin that would anger my Lord; so, swift unsure atonement with a forced smile, until the panic of displaying false remorse for irreverence dissipated. While the umbilical theology had been falling away, my God had been kicking at my heels, prompting *me* to entertain *Him;* I wasn't sure He liked jazz much; Devil's music. Not knowing the mind of a God whose debatable choices define every moral action causes *symptoms* of paranoia. *These* days, He seemed to be saying things I wanted to hear, speaking in *my* voice, with a Sussex accent, which makes sense if one takes the time to have a good long hard think about it, for, for a best-friend renowned for making stuff happen, it seemed the only things *I* could persuade Him to agree to make happen were things that I could already do, and did do, by my own blistered hand, within arm's reach, but that's *my* God for you.

Mulling upon the apocalypse causes *symptoms* of paranoia. Isolation causes *symptoms* of paranoia. Being with people causes *symptoms* of paranoia. Empathy causes *symptoms* of paranoia. Arriving late'n'flustered, sweaty'n'smelly; constricted in small spaces near sensitive sinuses causes *symptoms* of paranoia. Smoking in a no-smoking area causes *symptoms* of paranoia. Running out of effective medicine causes *symptoms* of paranoia. Withdrawal of an emotional crutch causes *symptoms* of paranoia. Susceptibility to superfluous belief causes *symptoms* of paranoia. Long-distance relationships cause the *symptoms* of paranoia. Short-distance relationships cause the *symptoms* of paranoia. Having: violent parents, loving parents, close parents, distant parents, strict parents, hippy parents, married parents, bigamous parents, divorced parents, a single parent, adopted parents, gay parents, no parents; parentage causes *symptoms* of paranoia. Cultivating blame'n'victimhood causes *symptoms* of paranoia. Having a big red shiny button to press, but not pressing it, despite every cell yelling to do so, causes *symptoms* of paranoia. Righteous anger badly directed causes *symptoms* of paranoia. Paranoid *symptoms* embody the inventive'n'creative process, from the view of the visionary, and armchair televisionary also.

A philosopher friend explained that: no *mental rearrangement* can be completed before *grandiosely* putting oneself out there out *there,* outside of one's myopic norm, conceptually, so as to be prepared for the inevitable brain change as'n'when it arrives. Conceptualism, found to be used as a common scientific tool after a childhood of Holy flapping, causes *symptoms* of paranoia. Self-betterment is often mistaken for *symptoms* of paranoia.

Lucid dreams'n'nightmares may cause *symptoms* of paranoia, or maybe *are* themselves the *symptoms* of paranoia, *maybe,* but, marijuana is widely advertised to *suppress* the recall of dreams, so it seems likeliest that *empirical data* should be the *root cause* of *those* particular sub-conscious expressions of understanding.

Holding love in one's heart causes *symptoms* of paranoia. Holding hate in one's heart causes *symptoms* of paranoia, etc., etc., etc. The accusation that weed causes *mental derangement,* back to the point, is tricky, nay, difficult, nay, nigh-on impossible, nay, *impossible* to prove amongst everyday hustlemusclebustle popping into mind from the invasive world of things'n'stuff, so, how one could assemble relevant info on the causes of *genuine* paranoia from anyone living a uniquely noisy modern life subjected to *symptoms* of paranoia at every second, all at once, from every direction, continually, until death, is quite fantastic.

Not to say that dope has no negative effects, to the contrary. Lethargy? Oh, yes. Agoraphobia? Oh, yes. Easy to anger? Oh, that'll be: hunger, caffeine, sugar, or any other drug, more likely. Undersharing? Oh, yes. Oversharing? Oh, yes. Prevarication? Oh, yes. A burden on friends? Well, no and yes, and yes'n'no. Paranoia? Oh, *I* don't know; *I* can't tell; what *feeds* normal?

Paralysed parrying paraphrased paradoxes, parochial parables loop in pertinent parenthesis; potted parallax opinions, plenty propitious to ponder profitably in private preoccupation, proper posers; parachronic pantisocratic pantheistic paralogisms, psychopathology, patois'n'pathos, appropriate compositional parataxis of piously pared paronomasia; spinning platitudes, preprepared parabolic peaks pirouette past improperly parsed.

Do you mean to say it'll *stop* wild thoughts, *ease* unbearable emotions, *and* cause death young *but later, and generate* wild thoughts, *provoke* unbearable emotions, *and* still cause death *but later?* Well, make a mix, or roll one up, let's get paranoid, baby.

Maybe the goal *isn't* peaceable; *maybe* the goal *is* self-harm; *maybe* the goal is to finally plunge that knife through one's chest. Or, *maybe,* the goal is to *not* self-harm violently, maybe sedation is the fastest route to repair but *you've* just tipped the nose below the horizon line. Never mistake a lack of movement for inaction. *I'm* no judge. *You're* no judge. Shut up. Nur-nur-n-nur-nur.

Nur-nur-n-nur-nur.
Nur-nur-n-nur-nur.
Nur-nur-n-nur-nur.
Nur-nur-n-nur-nur.
Nur-nur-n-nur-nur.
Nur-nur-n-nur-nur.
Nur-nur-n-nur-nur.
Nur-nur-n-nur-nur.
Nur-nur-n-nur-nur.
But it's not weed.
Nur-nur-n-nur-nur.
Nur-nur-n-nur-nur.
Nur-nur-n-nur-nur.
Nur-nur-n-nur-nur.
Nur-nur-n-nur-nur.
It cannot be weed.
Nur-nur-n-nur-nur.
Nur-nur-n-nur-nur.
Need some money.
Nur-nur-n-nur-nur.
Nur-nur-n-nur-nur.
Nur-nur-n-nur-nur.
Nur-nur-n-nur-nur.
Nur-nur-n-nur-nur.
Nur-nur-n-nur-nur.
Nur-nur-n-nur-nur.
WHAT'D YOU SAY?
Nur-nur-n-nur-nur.
Nur-nur-n-nur-nur.
Nur-nur-n-nur-nur.

Nur-nur-n-nur-nur.
Nur-nur-n-nur-nur.
Nur-nur-n-nur-nur.
I'm NOT paranoid.
Nur-nur-n-nur-nur.
Nur-nur-n-nur-nur.
Nur-nur-n-nur-nur.
Nur-nur-n-nur-nur.
Nur-nur-n-nur-nur.
Nur-nur-n-nur-nur.
Nur-nur-n-nur-nur.
Nur-nur-n-nur-nur.
Or, not *only* weed.
Nur-nur-n-nur-nur.
Nur-nur-n-nur-nur.
Nur-nur-n-nur-nur.
Nur-nur-n-nur-nur.
Nur-nur-n-nur-nur.
Nur-nur-n-nur-nur.
Nur-nur-n-nur-nur.
Have you got any?
Nur-nur-n-nur-nur.
Nur-nur-n-nur-nur.
Nur-nur-n-nur-nur.
Nur-nur-n-nur-nur.
Now I'm paranoid.
Nur-nur-n-nur-nur.
Nur-nur-n-nur-nur.
Nur-nur-n-nur-nur.
Nur-nur-n-oooooh,

Nur-nur-n-nur-nur.
Nur-nur-n-nur-nur.
Nur-nur-n-nur-nur.
Nur-nur-n-nur-nur.
Nur-nur-n-nur-nur.
Nur-nur-n-nur-nur.
Maybe a little bit.
Nur-nur-n-nur-nur.
Nur-nur-n-nur-nur.
Nur-nur-n-nur-nur.
Nur-nur-n-nur-nur.
Nur-nur-n-nur-nur.
Nur-nur-n-nur-nur.
Nur-nur-n-nur-nur.
Nur-nur-n-nur-nur.
Nur-nur-n-nur-nur.
Nur-nur-n-nur-nur.
Damn I've run out.
Nur-nur-n-nur-nur.
Nur-nur-n-nur-nur.
Nur-nur-n-nur-nur.
Nur-nur-n-nur-nur.
I wish I had some.
Nur-nur-n-nur-nur.
Nur-nur-n-nur-nur.
Nur-nur-n-nur-nur.
Nur-nur-n-nur-nur.
I CAN'T HEAR YOU.
Nur-nur-n-nur-nur.
Nur-nur-n-nur-nur.
ffuucckk oooofffffff.

part 2a

—

Fully Groan

UNIVERSITY OF LOVE pt.2

14: Nymphette

A local male friend often swung by to mourn our relationship disasters with a cup of tea and a sigh. We were both rubbish at love and would laugh loudly sharing our stories of romantic catastrophe. I valued those chats, having found a friend whose failures matched my own. We laughed'n'laughed, and laughed.

Out of the blue, but not unexpectedly, he started dating this crazy chick, a tiny blonde slip of a thing with more problems per cubic inch than anyone knew what to do with. Her answer was sex. She really wanted sex. Lots'n'lots. She soon moved into his place and smothered him in a blanket of pure desire.

He asked my advice about premature, well, you know, pre, you know, she's way too sexy and, well, you know, sort of type thing. I knew just what he meant, although was still hoping to talk myself into a position where I could get to learn to live with the embarrassment of it in company, that particular humiliation seemed fun. We guessed at possible delaying strategies together. He made me promise not to tell anyone, I never spoke a word.

While he spent time at college, she made herself known, calling by to chain-smoke cigarettes and drink tea as fast as the kettle would boil. I could see why he liked her, she was damaged, open, wild, a fragile urchin, a gypsy dame, said what she meant, there was no tricking her, she wouldn't have it. I learned much.

One drizzly afternoon, her boyfriend had promised to drop by on his way home for our regular chat. While still light outside there came a knock upon the door. The lock had barely clicked when *she* pounced through in silk, slinking her arms in'n'about, entwining her legs around mine. I stood firm, in concern, believing her to be deeply upset, until she started to *climb* me, like a feisty squirrel up a sleepy tree. Mwah mwah mwah. Uh?

As her tongue pushed its way mouthwards, spasms of shock and repulsion shook me from inaction. I pulled away and peeled her off, but she was upon me like a cat, toppling us dead weight to the floor. We spun'n'rolled until she let go sufficiently to extricate myself from her grip and get things between us, but up she jumped, chasing around the room; grabbing, groaning, scratching, catching, clutching, clasping, clenching, kissing madly, compressing her soft body parts against mine, grinding her delicately silk-clad rib-bones into any unwarily-extended limb.

With sofa-cushions as makeshift shields, I defended the stairwell using my longer frame to hold her head at arm's distance, pushing her away with ever increasing force until she fell to the floor with a disturbing crump, upturning the wobbly coffee-table.

She lay still. I thought I might've been responsible for her death, a fairly serious charge, and so briefly let down my guard in concern; whence she grabbed at my leg, slid her small hand up the inside of my shorts, and discovered her intended mark.

I froze for a few seconds, tumescent, unhurriedly processing the abomination of what was happening. How very interesting; *that* does *that*, oh, how marvellous is the wonder of biology, eh?

It took no more than the length of a deep breath to unclasp her hand, force her onto the sofa and roughly sit on her. Feminism be damned, little else could be done. There was no stopping this energetic love-ball from pressing'n'pecking with a loud mwah mwah mwah, spreading cheap scarlet lipstick over whatever passed nearest her face. Fragile squirmy arms would break free from fair-restraint to rub at an erogenous zone, and I'd *have to* squash her again, under soft sofa cushions, under me.

After an eternity she calmed down a bit and teased me about 'obvious' hang-ups, while I berated her for being in a relationship with a best chum, all the while cursing loudly the single girls in my life for not wanting this aspect of gleeful sin with me, when such a beautiful unavailable girl, that I couldn't have, did. Wah!

My housemate arrived home unannounced, burst through the door and took in the devastating scene. She got shy and, though I guided her to the front door, physically, not roughly, she ran upstairs instead. Relieved, more than anything else, I explained away the mess and outlined the goings on. He found it hysterical, naturally, which it was, kind of, *she* certainly was.

As I tidied up, wiping away the worst of the greasy lipstick, he went upstairs to piss, only to come back wide-eyed'n'blinking. You'll never guess what I just saw. What? Well, she wants it, *that's* for sure. *It?* It. *Really?* Really. *It?* Yes, it. *Sure?* Sure, she was asking for you. *Right,* I'm not bloody well going up there, that *is* for certainly bloody sure, her bloody boyfriend is only bloody well coming bloody round any bloody minute, would you please get rid of her. No way, you wanted my blessing, this is your chance. Please please please with a cherry on top. Um, no, with sauce'n'sprinkles, deal with your own shit. That's just it, I need a crap, urgently, a *bad* one. No. *Please.* No. *Pleeeease.* No. *Pleeeeease.* No. Oh, fuck you. No, fuck you. Grrrrr. Tea? Sure.

Neither he, nor me, would shoo that she from the house. If she were a bloke, we'd've had him out in a second, but girls, well, there are rules, or we believed there to be; a chivalrous code, detailing not to throw scantily clad women onto a city street. We heard a rhinoceros crashing about, things landing heavily. He went upstairs nervously to check that she wasn't dead, but came back with a report that she was now stark-naked *in* bed.

Knock knock knock. Fuck. Hello mate, you'd better come in.

I explained gently that his girlfriend was, at least partially, mentally unwell, and that she needed to be taken from the house immediately because I needed a crap, and couldn't go upstairs. Or words to that effect. He wasn't best pleased, to say the very *very* least; lipstick remained glued everywhere, he wasn't blind. He took her home without humour. We stopped our regular chats. Shame, this one would have made him laugh like a drain.

15: Groan Men

By all accounts, liberated women can be a hard bunch to please, just like liberated men, I'd never understood what all the fuss was about; we'd grown up under Maggie, Betty, and Lizzy, in *our* society there weren't any glass ceilings that *I* could see, because they're glass, obviously. To *my* untrained youthful eye there appeared to be nothing that *only* a free man *could* do which a free woman *couldn't,* as a free soul in a free country in this most blessed of eras, however, evidently, there was loads of stuff.

In amateur music, and all the amateur arts, we were at a stage where the only criteria for doing anything, functionally, was: turning up, and then doing it; *it* couldn't have been more equal without pills. Obviously, one required expensive equipment to start the whole process off, the internal desire to get involved, a *bit* of talent, free time to do whatever *it* is, and the financial clout to buy a drink at the social afterwards, or maybe two.

Within the capitalist system of musical instrument ownership, *anyone* could slink in unnoticed to play along with the double-bass section in *any* amateur orchestra; anyone *could* play *any* instrument should they wish to, in fact, there'd always been rather a predominance of women in orchestras I'd played in, and I *had* been looking. Anyone *could:* conduct, compose, write, draw, paint, dance, act, do *anything.* Oh, ah, maybe not *anything.*

A female pope remains unlikely. And there it is. *There's* the smudge on the glass ceiling. Religious patriarchy. Luke 23v28. *Ahem:* blessed are the wombs that never bore. Ahahaha-hur-hur-huh-huh-huh. Could *that* be true, pure, clean, Holy comedy? Would God laugh? I didn't *feel* capable of misogyny, it *must* be a humorous God allowing sexist words to get all muddled up into English as daft punnery like that. Yes, *that's* it. Effing words.

Men remain the bar by which comparison is set, due to stuff;
phenotypes, firm physiology stuff, big-chief first to feast stuff,
fiercest, fastest, fattest, toughest, fighting off a feral wolf stuff,
physiocracy, Rephaim, Nephilim, *prima facie* physiognomy stuff,
scuffles, kerfuffles, fisticuffs stuff, fending off gruff riff-raff stuff,
ferric forges, flaming furnaces, hefty forearms, physique stuff,
defending forts, kinsfolk, serfs, feuds, feoffments, fiefdom stuff,
farmsteads, crofters in fleeces, flocks in fallow fields stuff,
forceful fireman's lifts stuff, fortifiers of family edifices stuff,
faithful fullsome fertile fiancés, formalised forbearance stuff,
fishermen in fitted knit-frocks facing gale-force fourteen stuff,
thanatophobic finger-folding stuff, fearful feelings, fideistic stuff,
enfeebled fidgety stuff, infinite anthropomorphic reflection stuff,
fantabulous phantoms, phantasm stuff, baffling phenomena stuff,
fairy-tale fabrications stuff, mystifying, far-fetched fables stuff,
nymph stuff, elf stuff, faerie forests, fawns, Mephistopheles stuff,
diffusion of beliefs founded on Lucifer's fall from perfection stuff,
fashioned faultless, facsimiles of figuratively flawless form stuff,
female formed from'n'for forlorn fellow, filleted off-cut stuff,
floods, pharoahs, pharisees, prophets, prophecies fulfilled stuff,
Philippians 4v4, Philemon v4 stuff, Ephesians v4-5,4v5,14 stuff,
deified fictive foreign aphorism, fragmented paraphrased stuff,
fallible friary stuff, fabulist sophistry stuff, fallacious guff stuff,
felonious fantasts proliferating terrifying fraudulent flam stuff,
fundamentalist Fathers following profane justification stuff,
apocryphal metaphysical puffery enforced ferociously stuff,
frothing funghified forager folks, frog-familiars for proof stuff,
pitchfork stuff, fiery fate stuff, flogged, flayed, flagellation stuff,
futile falsified confession stuff, flattened, *peine forte et dure* stuff,
fiendish phallocentric stuff, foreskins, familial filiation stuff,
flammable stuff, in-fighting stuff, fanatic faction fervour stuff,
khalifate, fatiha, fatidica, fatwahs for fiction, fencing foil stuff,
sanctified defeat by falchion stuff, forbidden femininity stuff,

offensive stuff, reflexively theophobic stuff, reformation stuff, fuming blasphemous yoof stuff, foaming self-confidence stuff, floccinaucinihilipilificationalism stuff, xenophobic troofs stuff, free to offend stuff, unfounded safety stuff, fist, face, floor stuff, refutation of flawed lofty waffly stuff, prolific philosophical stuff, refined unfalsifiable stuff, purified by sufficient clarification stuff, scientific fact-finders flopping off of forty-foot floats stuff, seafarer stuff, fo'c's'les, futtocks, frigates for profiteering stuff, full-sail flotillas, forestays flapping, fore'n'aft fin-rudders stuff, fond farewells stuff, tomfool half-wits barfing off of ferries stuff, life-crafts, frail inflatables stuff, females'n'infants off first stuff, flotsam, floating far-off on flatulent rafts of putrefying stiffs stuff, dolphins, shark-fins stuff, flounder adrift, inefficient flailing stuff, fedoras affixed, fame'n'fortune, rifling franchise, trafficking stuff, flora'n'fauna stuff, useful fleshy fruits stuff, safari trophy stuff, furs, fangs, felines floored two-fold, elephant-foot furniture stuff, phylogeny, finches, flamingos, giraffes, buffalos, puff-adders stuff, puffer-fish in five-foot fish-bowls stuff, foolish unforgivable stuff, frightful stuff, awful stuff, horrific unlawful unfeeling stuff, unfunny stuff, foulest of filthy stuff, flesh suffering hateful stuff, fastened freemen flogged for farthings stuff, crestfalling stuff, infamous stuff, slothful figures flumped on fat fundaments stuff, reflective stuff, unfathomed faults confided in confessional stuff, stiff-upper-lip stuff, froggy coughs, forgiveness for pay-offs stuff, finance, funds, futures, portfolios, graphs, fiscal flux'n'flow stuff, foul profit forecast stuff, affording enough stuff stuff, thrift stuff, mafia stuff, fingers painfully fractured, bailiffs unruffled stuff, stupefyingly unfair stuff, manifestly fair stuff, Fabianism stuff, federal welfare stuff, leftie stuff, far-left stuff, stuff-as-theft stuff, feats of munificence stuff, affluence's effect on influence stuff, affecting effectual soft-influence, fitful cease-fire defense stuff, philanthropy stuff, foreign fund stuff, oil-fields, fuel for fire stuff, grief, strife, refugees fleeing from stuff, electrified-fence stuff,

coffin-fodder, futile conflicts, fifes, fanfares, fog of warfare stuff,
fleshbags on foothills for infantry officers to force forwards stuff,
fusillades confronted for fraught fleeting flagstaff freedoms stuff,
front-line flint-lock rifles, In Flanders Fields, floppy lifeless stuff,
afraid of foes stuff, fretful phobophobia, fleeing the draft stuff,
suffragettes framing faint-hearts for white-feather perfidy stuff,
from fat-fryer to gun-fire, fizzing phosphor stuff, fratricide stuff,
fascism, fylfot, führer, fritz, misfeasance fought in France stuff,
full-tilt Spitfires surfing updrafts at famous chiffon-cliffs stuff,
Faireys, Fairchilds, Flying-Fortresses, airforce forays flown stuff,
luftwuffe fleets, flakpanzers, die Fokkers und Fokke-Wulfs stuff,
finding foes have faces, families, friends, laugh at flatulence stuff,
farts'n'guffs stuff, funny'n'daft stuff, laughable, flatly farcical stuff,
pacifist stuff, enough is enough stuff, affiliated'n'different stuff,
fraternity, philandry, factious, fatuous, former-faculty fealty stuff,
favours, friends, snuff sniffed in stuffy offices off-Mayfair stuff,
four-finger stiffeners swiftly quaffed before'n'after golf stuff,
professional stuff, unprofessional stuff, flattery as function stuff,
faceless fulsome squiffy sycophantic fags fawning footly stuff,
affirmed affectations stuff, fashions followed, foppish fads stuff,
flamboyant flourishings of quiffs stuff, bouffant coiffure stuff,
flagons of fermented draft stuff, a swift half of craft in a fez stuff,
fiddle-faddle, piffling fiasco stuff, off the cuff, flossy fanciful stuff,
affable heartfelt stuff, feed the unfed, fun-runs for famine stuff,
steadfast stuff, feet-finding, fatherly footsteps to follow in stuff,
finials, flat-caps, ferrets, fitchews, pilfering a few pheasants stuff,
footy, flags unfurled, foot-long frankfurters, half of soft-fizzy stuff,
frozen by beautiful reflections stuff, flowerpot frutescent stuff,
fall facedown flush for flirtatious floosies in half-a-jiff flat stuff,
bumfluff, tufts of facial foliage stuff, find how far is *too* far stuff,
fascinating muff stuff, facile photographs, selfies-in-the-buff stuff,
frolicking, flanked by femurs, philanderers fleshly fondling stuff,
foxy bit of fluff stuff, fornication for fun, phalluses, fannies stuff,

filthy top-shelf stuff, prefer it freaky stuff, rough safe-word stuff, *folie a deux* stuff, *force majeure affaires*, *femme fatales* stuff, frustrating unfulfilment stuff, half-fluffed, furthers refused stuff, pheromones, foreplay, flaccid affections rebuffed frostily stuff, effectual fellatio, fluids on frock stuff, forgive'n'forgetful stuff, aftereffects, effortful refocus, unified fidelity, fortitude stuff, falsehood, flummery, favourite flowers, perfume, fancy gift stuff, forthright stuff, miffed, flying off in aloof puffy huffs stuff, furiously flung stuff, jiffy-bags aflame full of fresh effluent stuff, efforts to lift the face self-vilified stuff, foreseen defamatory stuff, plaintiff defense briefings finding former Freudian faults stuff, suffering forfeits stuff, frazzled, flipping fore-fingers up at stuff, flopping feet on sofa stuff, full fridge, indifferent to fat-free stuff, comfort food, fried stuff, French fancies, full-fat cream puff stuff, pharmaceutical stuff, puff puffed, sniff snuffed, foolhardy stuff, festival campfire stuff, flip-flops, falafels, finding oneself stuff, flowerbeds, green-fingers, fox-proof fences, self-sufficient stuff, faffing with backfiring Royal-Enfields, mid-life catastrophe stuff, refurbished crofts, transformed lofts stuff, surfer lifestyle stuff, foams off Fistral Beach stuff, flippers, muffin-top midriffs stuff, flares, colourful scarf, platforms, whiffy festering footwear stuff, funk, falsetto, deftly fast-fretting Fender finger-boards stuff, amplifier feedback stuff, deafened fans, fame for fifteen stuff, loafing in prefabs, sifting free foodstuffs, freeze-dried coffee stuff, dandruff, follicles failing, forehead fraying, fimbriated fuzzy stuff, stuff stuffed in drafts stuff, fabric filled floo, asphyxiation stuff, suffocating fumes stuff, final, fatal, effective efficient selfish stuff, defenestration, falling in front of traffic, fast shifting freight stuff, crucifix face-first flops off of four-story rooftops, brief relief stuff, funerals, phoning friends of friends, significant definitive stuff, and men shall remain the bar by which comparison is set, because men are competitive like that and would get cranky.

I knew stuff about women too; iffy stuff.

A fair fraction: half; everyone over two says as much. Aha.

As ever'n'always, society was living through great changes; burning bras, wonder-bras'n'that; women's lib had come'n'gone, and come again as glitzy girl-power; taking back *The Power;* celebrating the magnificent flowering of the feminine, this time, flopping'n'plopping out of low-cut lycra. I couldn't decide if an erotic appreciation of the female form by God-given desires could ever be considered as any part of feminism, whatever *that* meant.

It would be great if a polarisation of harmonious simultaneity existed in one beautiful definition; a 'Feminism' for all peoples of all nations, and none; of all genders, and none, and both, to use, but no, no such thing exists, *couldn't* exist, not in a 'free' society, for there's never going to be an agreed value on which aspect of femininity any member of the crowd *should* perceive as most immediately pertinent to the subject of debate, to fit personal empirical meta-dilemmas and rolling internal monologues that loop'n'hoop, pooh'n'pool; haughtily splitting the world in twain, half'n'half, and half again.

Impenetrable tangled knots of individualised generalism and universal exclusivity; diametrical signalling-poles all the way up. As with men.

Women say that feminism isn't about man-hating, which is a nice sentiment; as a man, I'm glad, however, if there *were* a feminist subsection on man-hating, specifically: nasty rapey men, then that there would be a thing that we could *all* agree on; nasty rapey men *are* a problem, nobody needs convincing of that.

Nasty-rapey-man-hating was my chosen specialty subject. Cocks. I'd refined indignation into pure distilled disgust, *my* wild hatred toward nasty rapey men equalled *anyone's* wild hatred; *my* feral fury at nasty rapey men equalled anyone's feral fury, there could be no reason why I shouldn't be able to stand up and join in the good fight for what's long been *seen to be* a woman's issue, as a free soul in a free country in this most blessed of eras.

I'm with *you,* sisters. I think you'll find that sisters are doing it for themselves, thank you very much. I'm still with *you,* sisters. Yes, why *are* you here? I'm with *you,* sisters, to support in any way you feel that I can help. Well, start by taking your passive aggressive nonsense away. I'm with *you,* sisters, from a distance and without action. Which proves what a useless inept lump you always were. I'm with *you* sisters, power to your elbow. Are you looking at our elbows? Only to check for unwanted men, *honest.* Are you saying women can't look after ourselves? No, I'm sure you could take on anything. So, you're saying it's a fair fight between a man'n'woman? Well, no. So, you *are* saying that women *are* weak. Um, I just want to help, go girl power. Oh, *right,* so you're a *perve.* No, I'm, um, well, alright, yes; an *aesthete,* but I promise to look you in the eye, and not at your bra-straps, or anything. But we can see you peeking through your fingers. Er, what if I said I were gay? What's that you say, you're gay? Um, it was a theoretical question. Ah, look, bless him, he's *shy.* Erm, but, er, I'm... Oh, thank God, get 'em out for the shy gay lad girls; get yer tits out, out out out, get yer tits out, out out out, geeeeet yer tits out, geeeeet yer tits out, geeeeet yer tits out for the shy gay lad. ...I'm *not* gay. Ooooooh, he's so sweet when he's angry. Okay, I'm still *not* gay, but I *am* a feminist. No, you're *not* a feminist, *I'm* a feminist, on account of being female and *unable* to rape women. Sure, but I'm *also* a feminist, a *male* feminist. No, *they* don't exist, unless, of course, you *are* gay. Um, er, well, that's not quite true, gay-men can be nasty'n'rapey too. You are an illiberal chauvinist of the highest order. Um, maybe, but I'm still a feminist. No, *I'm* a feminist. Sure, but I'm *also* a feminist. No, *I'm* a feminist. Sure, but I'm *also* a feminist, a *man-hating* feminist. Aha, feminism isn't about man-hating. Well, maybe it *should* be. No, it should not, and I should know, *I'm* a feminist, *I've* got a vagina. Okay, *fine,* well, I suppose I'll have to be a patriarch then, is there an application form that needs filling in?

UNIVERSITY OF LOVE pt.2

16: Snap

The pilot suggested that we jointly Musical Direct a show for the Uni Musical-Theatre lot. It seemed a load of responsibility and turning up for nothing to me, so I declined. He said, there'll be dynamic teenage girls. I'm in, said a nearby mouth. Dammit.

As co-MD, auditioning the male leads, options were *so* very *very* poor, that I put myself forward for an acting part instead; the bumbling comedy relief; it was a shoe-in. Exhilarating stuff.

My new role meant lots of grinning goofily one step behind proceedings, something that came naturally; something to own as part of myself, wholesale. Butt. Hammy acting, bitty line-learning, croaky-singing, stage-upsetting; all *so* awry, I ruined the show. The other actors knew it, an unseen muttering chorus knew it, bored technicians knew it, cringing audiences knew it, the parents when they came all the way up from Sussex to see it knew it, my pilot knew it, the pit-band knew it, even *I* knew it, although, I'd have to live with it, so I pretended not to notice.

As the shows passed by in a blur of subsidised lager, a graceful stage technician, gently flirtatious throughout the run, made obvious extra efforts to hang out with our clique. We connected. She, laughing loudly in the wings whenever I attempted humour. Perfect. Easily impressed, with *very* low standards. Excellent. Hoorah. Next chapter now defined. Tingle tingle tingle. Teehee.

At the end of the week, at the after-show party, we caught one another's smiley eyes as we circulated, gradually homing in on each other, not *too* obviously, *obviously*. Having done the rounds a bit, we were hanging out at the back, chatting, laughing, flirting shyly through a musky blush of rare courage, when an unknown assailant twisted my drink hand into a thumb-lock, *smash,* and hauled my baulking bulk towards the dance floor by the blisters.

Dmcha dmcha dmcha. In the blare of screaming mechanicals cones of vision fell on the tall guy nursing his arm in the middle, wincing'n'sneezing amid a smog of eye-watering *eau des oignon*. Oi, oh, wow, look at you, good hair, look, I'm not a dancer, and you, um, you spilled my drink and, sorry, but: who are you? Dmcha dmcha dmcha. *What?* Quizzically painted brows implied.

She, an apparently tall girl of huge hair, thickly rouged lips, and a scent which covered mine; nowt else was discernible in the heady din. She angered me greatly by yelling at full force into delicate eardrums directly in front of deafening speakers; indistinct indecipherable vowels without meaning. ...PLEASE STOP SHOUTING. Silence. Slow dance? *Not likely!* As I made to run, she grabbed, held, insisted, and *I* couldn't punch *her* in the face.

Poking out in all the right places, she just went ahead and pressed those places against *my* abdomen, powerfully wrapping my reticent arms around her sand-glass waist as décolletage and fumes filled widening-eyes. The stirrings of a great soup gurgled below as she pushed in closer, squashing in pelvis to pelvis, rocking us forcefully back'n'forth to a terrible heartfelt wailing.

I stared over massive hair into the soft grey eyes of the gentle technician gazing back sourly, mopping at the floor. Our moment broke off distracted as my clench-fisted hands were placed upon buttocks, digits scraped open, open-sores tapped down onto polyester, the lot. Cold grey eyes stalked out of the hall, deadpan.

It was possibly my tumid penis that spoke to me, the voice said, this is okay, stay here. God couldn't do a thing about it.

She led the way back to my house and jumped my bone, bouncing around with back arched and top off, whirling her bra around her head, enjoying herself immensely, a cowgirl in the throws of rodeo. Wow. Better than I'd ever imagined it; hot, sweaty, steamy, good old-fashioned squelching. She shrieked, yelped, gasped, ground away, wrenched about from side to side, and snapped my cock.

Seconds in, it all had to cease, now, immediately, at once, instantly. Stop, I said. She didn't want to stop. No, I said, pulling away to medically tend; admonishing her sexual enthusiasm, which didn't sit too comfortably. Quick, get ice. *You* get ice. *Please* get ice. *You* get ice. Get ice NOW, *pleeeeeeeeeease*, if you'd be so kind. What the hell, man? *Nnnnnngh*. You're out of ice.

A proud wine-red crescent half-way up around one side, acutely sore to the touch; chronic pain passed through the balls, down the legs, back up through the arse, spine, neck'n'head; deflating tissue an agony-magnet, sucking in pain from demonic dimensions, inverting the total inexplicable joy thus far achieved into a singularity of singular self-pity. Curled up, bent double under the low splashy toilet, drenched in cold wet towels like a beached dolphin, delirious nausea overcame all else; retching, spinning, bowels hanging off the shower-rail and all about.

Okay, God, You win, I'm listening now.

So that was that for a while; flinching to the touch, purple-blue from base to tip, a violent violet smudge quickly turning through green to black to red, a raised ridge of permanent kinky change.

Although scared of this whirlwind of a woman, I *was* keen to pursue this, she wanted to make whoopee, and *with me*, hoorah, there's no turning *that* down. Once healed, we'd certainly be at it like rabbits, but, *ow*, for now, the ow, the ouch, the very thought.

Before it'd repaired sufficiently, she'd arrive Saturday nights, late, a little tipsy, to eat me up, beat me up, bruise the damaged piece by landing on a delicate lap without due care'n'attention.

Once or thrice I convinced her to sit on my face, which I was particularly happy about, not to have to worry about raw hands or gland, or glans. She wasn't overly comfortable with it, being more into penises, but she'd still clamp her muscular thighs around my ears as I'd inexpertly apply willing to the new task. Tumescence throbbed painfully below as I'd reach up to jiggle her excellent titties. Bucket-list item fulfilled. Tick. Ow. Untick.

UNIVERSITY OF LOVE pt.2

17: In for a Penny

Life changed. Rent pulled, as a magician's tablecloth, without a table. Having told the parents I'd not been to college in a while, they thought that tough love would probably be for the best.

No education, no rent; no rent, get a job. *That's* the deal.

Sadly, for me at least, my last available penny had been spent on a smashed pint, still mulled upon resentfully. Luxuries gone; gigs too rare to justify rehearsal; busking: subject to northern weather and playing partners, my podgy angel had vanished, and guitarists are such a delicate bunch. Time to change the dream.

Outside in the world, many 'jobs' were tried, immediate start, pyramid stuff, all awful. When knowingly being shafted; while hungry and with rent added to responsibility, it is hard to walk out of the door and leave a potential pay-day under an onslaught of neurolinguistic programming from slick people in shiny suits in bright offices, while still owing the company for a branded bag, or trousers, or whatever they'd used to trick you into owing them money for wasting your time while looking for a real job.

As a business model, selling cheap clothing to a stream of desperate paupers seemed to be doing well. It seemed obvious that many of these companies would go bust unless they had a high turnover of 'staff', in which case they'd be fine, distracting the uneducated masses from suicide with clever business-speak and seemingly pointless tasks. Once I'd worked out what was what, having amassed a fairly decent collection of unwearable embroidered polo-shirts, some still owing today, I'd walk myself, and a few others, out of first-day 'training-sessions' boisterously, when the expensive merchandise required to be purchased by all company 'employees' had been brought out as a precursor to working a week, or two, or more, for free. Bye. But. Bye.

A job that paid regularly, where keenness would be valued, guaranteeing more than a-pint-an-hour, now required yesterday. Out every morning with soggy dog-eared papers, every shop, club, and open doorway, getting home worse off as rent amassed; no cash, no drink, no smoke, no music, no erection, no bending.

All the most poorly paid desk-jobs required a qualification in some other subject than jazz. I wished, again, briefly, that I'd not *gone* to bloody music college, and then wished that I'd not *left* bloody music college, but then: a thought struck out of the blue.

Next day, off I hirpled into town, through town, bishbashbosh, a little bit of pleading'n'flirting with the manager, and I'd landed a part-time hourly-paid job at the vibeless café. Good things come to those who wait, clean up, and make'n'serve sandwiches, over those waiting to rehearse. The wait for a shift began. Tick.

On the way home in a scabby suit, I popped into the local pub and asked the spherical landlord, sat on his three stools, possibly permanently, if he'd got *any* shifts starting immediately for a keen, needy sort. Yur'kay, he wheezed, coughed'n'spluttered.

Weekend pub shifts; clothed in polo-shirt and water-proof trousers that pinched the bruised member: in for a pound, I'd put in for a pinny. Open blisters took the steamy beer dousing as open sores do: eyes'n'fingers wept remorselessly, but hey ho. Smile slapped on, sodden fraying fingers wrapped in ribbons of useless plasters, it wasn't long before I'd become the very best glass-collector that pub ever knew; king of ashtray emptying.

Three long weekends later, I still owed them for the polo-shirt and cock-rubbing trews, being paid off at *less* than a pint an hour, *before* tax-taken although none was owed, *and* the first weekend was for *free.* I'd not agreed to that, *surely,* and nearly argued myself out of any job at all before having taken a penny, but still, it bunged a leak not haemorrhaging time'n'money as a full-time amateur musician; plus, we'd get a bottle of beer at shift's end; cold'n'crisp, frosty'n'free, thirst-quenching economy lager.

TV licensing had been round several times, overdue bills for the power, gas, water, and now rent threatened broken fingers: various other financial problems stuck in the craw, wah, blah. My pilot had inherited a large amount of cash from a dead uncle's estate and gone on holiday for a week with a girl. Envious was I; I wished *my* relatives would die and leave me some money, for about a millisecond, before hating myself for the perversion of wishing such a thing, and then rewishing that all values of society weren't upside-down so as to force good people to consider such a foul abomination of thought at least once in their otherwise innocent lives, however briefly. Bloody society.

On my twentieth birthday, I took the day off panicking about money. Hurrah. The rent can wait, time is fleeting. So I took a pay-envelope to the local shop and got a packet of proper cigarettes, beer, and something strong. Twenty Bennies, a slab of lager and a bottle of vodka, it'll have to do. Hey guys, party at mine, spread the word. I stashed the vodka in my room, removed the wobbly coffee table, a drummer set a drum-kit, a violinist appeared, we opened the door'n'windows, and passed the best part of the day making as much racket as possible, a beer to any passing musician who'd stop'n'play. If ever there would be a good moment to die, I thought, enriched with rare rhythm, *this* would be it; rolling in debt, a great little party, at least two-dozen people likely to turn up to the funeral, any moment now. Now.

When we finally stopped playing, all the beer had been drunk and someone had nicked the voddy. People buggered off and I was left with an ear, nose'n'throat infection the likes of which kill, but no such luck. *That's* for wishing for an inheritance. I took decongestant on the poor advice of a musical-theatre smoking-buddy, drying up any mucus that might've alleviated the acute dry pain. Calls were made to beg soup and *real* medicine; double debt piles mounted as favours were spent. A week later, in bed with fever, a first shift at the vibeless bar passed-by, apparently.

18: Sausage Rolls

Saturday night was *her* night, the night she loved to go out, to get drunk, and 'get' 'some' 'cock', as she put it, which became awkward when I couldn't satisfy this need, so, instead, moral codebook in hand, I freed her as a modern man should, insisting she go 'get' any 'cock' she wanted to while I healed, and, if she *did* 'get' 'some' 'cock', I'd be okay with that. The hippy in my heart did an inward little dance, clicking the heels, bursting with pride for doing the right thing, for once. She said that she only wanted *my* 'cock', my *broken* 'cock'. It all got a bit fraught. No one likes outright rejection; for certain, neither of us did. Selectively deaf to my complaints of exhaustion that troughed beyond midnight, she'd still swing by in the early hours, committed to her task. Don't sit there, ow, sit here. Points at face, grins sheepishly.

Blood-flow brought nausea, bagsful, the whole body rejected the fleshly imagery filling the vision, instead, opaque periphery of thudding opalescence overtook all; catching the head in a door while beating the bollocks with a bag of bricks'n'billiard balls. Eyes had to be averted from her youthful curvaceous form, focus of mind specifically meaty, mindless, joyless'n'sexless.

Is there something wrong with your eyes? Nnmmph. Look at me. Nnnnmmph. Open your eyes. Mmmmbrbrbrrrrrhumnm. Oh, yeah, there, nearly, back a bit, a bit less, a bit more, theeere. Hnghahhhaaaaahhhuurp, Ican'topenmyeyesyou'resosexyithurts mmhmmhmmhmmmmmf, aaaaaaaaaaooooooooooooooowwwww.

Overcome with eventual orgasms she would lay puffing, laughing, cooling off as it dried into the sheets. Life owed me these sticky moments of near death by fanny asphyxiation later on in life, not now for crying out loud, later, or earlier, just not now ow ow ow ow ow uuuuurrrgh. I'm gonna sleep in the bath.

We made efforts to meet outside of the bedroom; both busy surviving, a post-pay-day date was set and it soon rolled round.

I left the house early, a little late, unburdened and ravenous. On the way to her house, hobbling along a path never previously followed, I passed by a quaint bakery in the old style. Through the smudged window, meagre pickings looked a bit fly-eggy, but the price was good and a plump jolly lady was arriving with a fresh tray, so I popped in and bought a piping-hot sausage roll. Thanks love. No, thank *you*. Ding.

Maybe I hadn't eaten rich food in a while; maybe magic flowed in that kitchen, whatever, that sausage roll remains the best ever pastry ever created anywhere ever. I had a full-body mouthgasm, and then another, uunnngh mmmhmmm. Stuffing the last into my pie-hole, with crumbs spitting'n'spilling, I marched straight back in to demand a dozen more; thirteen, as it should be. Thanks love. Nngh, fang *ynngh*. Ding.

Munching through a further few, middle distance came'n'went, bouncing along the sunny side, honeysuckle sweet on the breeze.

Upon arrival, she wasn't ready, so she let me in, introduced her housemates, then disappeared upstairs. Uuuuuuh, hi, er, oooooh, yes, here, these are amazing, would you like one? Um, what are they? Ah, glad you asked, they're the best sausage rolls in Yorkshire, try one. What are they made of? Well, they're pretty heavy on the grease. What's in it? Oh, I dunnow, are there laws against Lincolnshire sausage in Yorkshire? No, what's the meat? Oh, er, sausage mince, maybe pork, maybe a bit of beef or something. No thanks. But you've not tasted... No, thanks. Oh, go on, have a taste. No, stop. Ooooooh, you're missing out, what about you? What? Want one? Want one what? Sausage roll. What are they made of? Well, they're pretty greasy. No, what's the filling? Er, Lincolnshire. No, what's the meat? Oh, er, pork, maybe, not sure, hah, might be cat, I dunnow, what do cats taste like? No thanks. Shame, hello puss puss, oh, ah, is this your cat?

When she came down, her housemates stood in a group around the door, staring. We left together, I, full of greasy meat, she, an eyeful, popping out of her top, as fragrant as a freshly peeled orange stuffed into the nostrils with a carving fork.

Oh, wow, look at you, you're, really, quite, short, aren't, you? Heels, I could go'n'get some if you want. No, it's, er, it's, um, fine, I'd just, convinced, myself, oh, never mind; *that* was all a bit odd. *What* was all a bit odd? That. What? *That,* in there, I'm not sure your housemates like me. No, of course they like you, they're lovely. Oh, well, they didn't wanna connect. Why'd you say that? Well, they didn't take *ohoho*, nearly forgot, would you like one of these? What are they? They are, *ahem,* the world's greatest ever *ever* sausage rolls. What are they made of? Well, they're mostly grease to be honest. No, what's the meat? I'm fairly sure it's pork. Ah, okay, you *are* aware that the entire house is Jewish? Er, um, erm, oh. You do know that *I'm* Jewish? Well, yes, but, um, er, the um, the er, the erm, the *sex* thing. What of it? Uh, well, uh.

I put down my moral codebook, it was of no use here.

Glottal stops and unalphabetisable nervous gurgles burbled from a phlegmy neck-hole as throat filled with stomach, which, in turn, topped up a park bin. Reliving the reactions in excruciating detail, several big thoughts struck me far dumber'n'number than usual; after which, blood drained and humour evaporated, until only shame remained; shame without comedy, or air.

Vertigo reeled as the ground split asunder to swallow my soul in unearthly fire; I shook, trembling in fear, penitently clearing an unforgivable sin before God. If He'd chosen that exact moment to return in His Majesty to sort innocent from sinner, there'd've been no chance to make amends, which would've been really *really* shit. Of course, if the rapture *had* happened, I'd've found out if God has a sense of humour, as we all would've; all at once discovering what God thinks of eating pigs *not* fed on excrement in a desert, years after He'd troubled to invent the fridge'n'all.

It had been my experience that bacon sandwiches, hog-roasts, hot-dogs, pork-pies, and all, had long-served as a guilty foodstuff among culturally blessed friends; not dire enough to care about, if anything, a well-rehearsed conversation piece. Oh, but, I really *really* shouldn't, ah, well, but, oh, fuck it, go on then, I am a really *really* rubbish: Rasta, Jew, Muslim, vegetarian, vegan, dieter, etc.

As far as I was aware, Holy Law didn't specifically prevent *me* eating *anything,* I knew that Jesus had renounced something on my behalf; I vaguely recalled some speech about not needing to wash the hands before eating, but pork? Had Jesus okayed pork? As a hardened omnivore, I remained grateful to *all* sentient life in the food chain, sacrificed that others may live; that *I* might live; now, penitent on jelly legs, I offered up a prayer, fearing the fates of all piggy-souls in the spectral pig-pen of porky purgatory.

Thank you pigs, all pigs of history; thank you for the creatures you've sustained by giving up your lives; thank you on behalf of any graceless sorts who've snuck slices of your flesh and not had a relevant porcine-friendly God to thank; thank you pig-farmers; thank you abattoir workers; thank you meat-factory workers; thank you butchers; thank you chefs; thank you Denmark, generally; thank you pigs that made it all the way to sausage rolls only to then be thrown up in a park bin; thank you all. Ah, pigs.

No wonder her house-mates had been disdainful. They must have thought me an impish demon sent to taunt'n'tempt them with forbidden food, or maybe they thought that their housemate was dating an uncultured idiot; either way, they were right, and were all owed a warm'n'heartfelt confession of arseheadedness, though I didn't plan to show my arsehead round there ever again.

In my defence, we'd been trained to *not* point at dissimilarity between peoples of the world by the act of *not* pointedly announcing differences. In mind's eye, realisation dawned that the highest hippy ideal, to ignore variables entirely, causes a social-blindness, as defined by levels of ignorance newly achieved.

Speaking as a lone soul set on a traumatic pathway toward integrity of mind, or death, whichever came first; as one in process of rejecting all certainty implanted in childhood, as one distanced from family faith in a very real sense by every 'immoral' act undertaken with leaden heart; as one dismantling half-truths'n'overlapping laws by any means likely *outside* of the familiar realm of scripture; as one in bedlam, pandemonium, chaos, uproar'n'indecision, I coveted her brazen *regard* for God's rules, as well as her flagrant *disregard* for the very same.

She freshly fascinated me in a way that I'd not noticed before; I wanted to study her, psycho-analyse her, peer in through the carefully crafted cosmetic mask and clouds of sinus-frying vapours to the complex befreckled human being hidden beneath. Parasite, lost in her eyes, when before I'd stared straight through. She'd become my super-heroine; her superpower: to bravely put her immortal soul on the line without concern for her own sanity. How a culturally religious person could, simultaneously, follow Holy Law for the one activity, and hold liberated views *without guilt of sin* for another *prohibited* activity, and without schizophrenia, or ever questioning the motive, baffled me utterly; *my* attempted adultery burned a hole 'tween heart'n'mind.

Firmly I insisted upon discussion of these holey issues, it was super important to me to be able to fill in some blanks, work out how she'd come to her decisions, and grow with her as my common-sense catalyser, but she wasn't interested in being a religious guidance councillor if I wasn't interested in penetrative sex, and I wasn't, not without an ice bath ready; not even then. Glumpf. Ow. That she wouldn't address the hypocrisy in our combined inconsistent ethics upset me deeply. Obviously the levels of hypocrisy were stacked one on top of the other infinitely, but, in this particular instance, defining our differences would avoid bigger issues of the highest social consequence, and so, I said so, and then again, then again'n'again, and again.

As big brains took over the reigns, I could start to talk to her without collapsing in a pained heap; we'd discovered a theme of common interest, or *I* had, for, far more important than our shared frustrated non-sex-life, *most* importantly, was to discuss the rôle of the scriptures in her life to discover which they were; to find out which laws we *both* used would be a total game changer. However, she still just wanted cock. Ecclesiastes 12v4.

Why're *you* back again? *You're* mental. Well, *you're* just a silly *silly* simile. You don't even know what that means. *Metaphor?* You'll learn something one day, then you'll be embarrassed by every word you ever spoke. But do *you* speak for God? Yes. *Yes?* Yes. Okay, good, well, while you're here, I've a *few* questions, so, if my God *is* Jehovah, and Allah is the same, why am *I* allowed bacon bits? Jesus? Seems like a bit of a heavy sacrifice for gammon steaks; God didn't send down his only son to die for bangers, and yet, there was something in Jesus' story and teachings that affected the nation's diet, caused embarrassment, vomiting, and a good deal of social unease too, so, for the sake of not repeating cringeworthy situations, God's finger was required. Leviticus 11v7-8, Deuteronomy 14v8, Isaiah 65v4. Then Jesus; Romans ch14, 1 Corinthians 10v25, 1 Timothy 4v3-5. Phew.

Unsure of the various chapters'n'verses that had produced *her* personalised theosophy, *fairly* certain that they'd never existed, we needed to study The Bible together, for, with another fifty years of life to suddenly think about seriously, I didn't want to wake up one day to find out that I was married to a religious nut, or that *she* was. If we were going to make a child at some point, which seemed inevitable the way she kept on, then I needed her to be onboard with the idea that: we didn't get to *keep* out-of-wedlock ungodly antics, but then hold onto, say, chopping at our child's genitals with a sharpened stone. We shouldn't get to pass on public declarations of *faith* for our progeny, unless to: *reject* Holy Decree, and officially *accept* unholy vice, or vice versa.

My demand for religious integrity entered the bedroom. Atop heaps of issues, the desire to fulfil *her* satisfaction could not be found; unresponsive to her sexual needs, brain farts farted; stifled by clouds of over-thinking. Health improved no end, as I *insisted* that she wouldn't get an orgasm until after we'd talked. She didn't like that much, claiming I was making too big a deal of it, maybe not fully aware that religious honesty would be the key to my staying sane, and a keystone to future happinesses.

Hoist by my own placard, theology be damned, I wanted her to join me in the agnostic frontier, where all scripture and association thereof had been extricated as rules to live by, *or, I'd've* needed to become Jewish. God had been preparing me for the snip, I'd've barely noticed the operation; now or never.

She told me she didn't much care for that 'silly old nonsense'; that same 'silly old nonsense' that had made me physically sick due to the offence having been caused by it; that same 'silly old nonsense' that thieves billions of children of an honest moral compass; that same 'silly old nonsense' which wastes trillions of young hours separating out that which is true, from: that which is *True;* that same 'silly old nonsense' which maintains a patriarchal system that all menfolk *would* feel ashamed of, if they weren't hog-tied to it while blamed as being the cause of it, unable to proffer solutions or opinions on how to give up such bad ideas as overlap feminism, *that* same 'silly old nonsense'.

Eventually I ran from her. I couldn't bring myself to say no, nor yes neither, so, I ran'n'hid, as rehearsed. Saturday night; home late, lights off, silence. Knock knock knockety knock. Shhhhh.

The last time I smelled her perfume was at a house party, when I hid behind the bed in the room with the coats in it while my musical theatre smoking buddy batted her away with small talk and 'no knowledge' of my whereabouts, a good chum. Suppressing a sneeze, I squeezed my cowardly brain so hard that I might well have become invisible by sheer force of will.

19: Tick

Staring out at the dank vibeless bar from behind the beer taps, I'd started imagining that *this* was *my* cold Hell, and I the demon whose task it was to pour boiling water into the begging mouths of these poor tormented souls forever; here'n'hereafter, recruited into Satan's eternal infernal daemonic catering corps; double shifts until apocalypse. Breaking down the barriers of the clock, dividing up the days, winding down empty distraction into: hour, half-hour, fifteen, ten, five, one-minute, one-second increments of insufficient monetary value to cover outgoings *before* fun. Tick.

The busy road looked tempting, I studied the traffic-flow for a likely spot to get the job done properly. Any day now; *now*. Tick. Now. Tick. One small cup of herbal tea coming up. Now. Tick.

Without warning, the podgy bari-playing angel wandered in unannounced wearing a great big grin, and bought a full pint with a high-denomination note. Looking about himself furtively, he relayed the events of his missing months; the bailiffs who'd taken *his* saxophone when collecting on a *housemate's* debts; running out on college-fees when the sums were more than he could borrow; tale after weepy tale of pecuniary worry'n'woe, which thoroughly cheered me up. I told him about my broken cock and the sausage rolls, but he didn't laugh, no one ever did.

After his second pint had been poured, and I'd wiped some tables'n'stuff, he told me he'd become a clown, joined a troupe, and had been living the good-life in a circus, seeing the world, meeting people, paid to make music; they'd recently hauled up in a nearby town for the week but were soon to hit the road, to tour Scotland over the summer season for hard'n'filthy lucre.

Oh, mate, I'm so happy for you, that all sounds utterly brilliant. Ja, es ist, so, du vonna job, or vot, hmmmmm? Hmmmmm.

Printed in Great Britain
by Amazon